Think big & take action!

D-LS

Limited Edition
Pre-published manuscript

Adviser Secrets

How To Become a Top Performer

A Guide to the 13 Most Important Communication
Skills Used by Top Performers

Dennis Sommer
CEO, Executive Business Advisers

iUniverse, Inc.
New York   Bloomington

Adviser Secrets How to Become a Top Performer
A Guide to the 13 Most Important Communication Skills Used by Top Performers

Copyright © 2008 by Dennis Sommer

iUniverse books may be ordered through booksellers or by contacting:

iUniverse
1663 Liberty Drive
Bloomington, IN 47403
www.iuniverse.com
1-800-Authors (1-800-288-4677)

Because of the dynamic nature of the Internet, any Web addresses or links contained in this book may have changed since publication and may no longer be valid. The views expressed in this work are solely those of the author and do not necessarily reflect the views of the publisher, and the publisher hereby disclaims any responsibility for them.

ISBN: 978-0-595-52344-3 (pbk)
ISBN: 978-0-595-62399-0 (ebk)

Printed in the United States of America

Also By Dennis Sommer

49 Marketing Secrets (that work) To Grow Sales (contributing author)

Dedication

In memory of my mother, Priscilla,
who inspired me to honest and kind to others.

To my wonderful family; Janis, Rachel, Kyle,
Kermit, Norma, Cindy, Samantha and Alexis.

You are always there to support my business ideas
and remind me family comes first.

Contents

Preface

After working in consulting, sales and business development for over 20 years, I've become very frustrated with the lack of originality in business books, training classes and seminars. I believe it's time for a new way of thinking, a new approach for handling complex business and professional development issues. For this reason, I started a company whose mission is to dramatically elevate business and professional performance by developing and implementing creative strategies that are innovative and action oriented. The solutions we provide are driven by our mission and help business owners, CEO's and executive management teams maximize business results.

If you are like most of my clients, your goal is to become the best in your industry. Maybe you want your business to have the largest market share. Perhaps you want to have the largest sales revenue. Maybe you want to be the best known and sought after in your profession, or collect the largest billing rate per hour. Possibly you are looking to advance within your company with the ultimate goal of becoming the CEO. Everyone with one of these goals wants the same thing. They want to become a top performer in their profession.

So, how do you become a top performer?

A New Creative Approach

I have developed a unique system to help my clients become top performers. This system is called the "Adviser Success Model" which is described in Chapter 2. The "Adviser Success Model" is a framework of guidelines and actions that help you focus on the client's needs, expectations and the value you can deliver. It is a complete approach covering planning and preparation, understanding client needs, delivering a valuable solution and nurturing your client relationship. This new and unique approach to business is turning average performers into top performers.

One of the most important elements in the "Adviser Success Model" is exceptional client communication. I call this the foundation for your success. You can be the smartest technician in your profession, but if you can't clearly articulate your recommendations to a client you will fail. This is why I have dedicated this entire book on key client communication skills used by top performers.

This Book is Different

Like you, I have read countless books on communication skills. I have attended the best training sessions and popular seminars on the topic. Afterwards I am disturbed by what I've seen and read. What's disturbing is most of the material fell into one or more of the following categories:

- Theory: material was theoretical and never applied to real life situations
- Non-actionable: material did not provide actionable advice
- Superfluous content: material entailed unnecessary detail, often 200 pages on one topic that could have been covered in one chapter
- Highly specialized: material was highly specialized in one industry or profession; therefore it was difficult to apply/relate the material to my particular needs.

My goal is to drastically change how information is delivered in books, training and seminars. Some say I am giving away the closely held secrets of top performers. The information I provide, if properly implemented, paves a winning roadmap or blueprint on how to become successful. My goal is to turn every one of my clients into a top performer.

To achieve my goal, I have developed this book and supporting material in a way that delivers information rarely seen in other books. You will find:

- field tested material used daily by top performers;
- step-by-step actions you can start tomorrow;
- concise materials organized into easily read chapters;
- compelling ideas that you can apply to any industry or profession.

Are you ready to get on the road to success?

Are you ready to become a top performer?

Let's start our journey now!

Introducing a New Approach

Imagine being in the top 1% of your profession - what I call a top performer. You are making more money than you could ever imagine. You spend a good portion of your workday at your beachfront mansion, on the golf course, or on your yacht. Your clients and peers look up to you as the "go to" person when times are tough. You don't work to cultivate clients; instead they are calling you day and night. You are receiving numerous awards, "Business Person of the Year", "Consultant of the Year", "Salesperson of the Year" and "Community Leader Award". It doesn't feel like work. You're having the time of your life. Every day is an exciting adventure. Even with all this success you find yourself spending more quality time with your family. Your business and personal life is in balance. It can't get any better.

Does this sound like a dream? Maybe today, but it could be your reality.

My goal is to help you become a top performer in your profession.

Are You Ready to Become a Top Performer?

Is a top performer more intelligent than you? Are they luckier? Were they just born to be a top performer? I say "no" to all the above. The difference is they decided to change. They decided to do things differently than everyone else. The status quo was not good enough. They decided to think in a creative, non-traditional way, thus implementing strategies to exceed their goals.

If you can't imagine yourself changing your current professional practices or not conforming to the "wisdom" provided in conventional business texts, then this book is not for you.

Are you still with me? Great. That means you are ready for change. Your mind is open for proven new creative ideas to help you become a top performer. Some of these new ideas might seem a drastic change from what you are doing today. You might think they are completely crazy. Don't worry! These are normal feelings. Just remember, these are the successful secrets held closely by top performers and, if you implement them properly, they will work for you too.

A Critical Success Factor

By far, communication skills are undeniably one of the most important skills mastered by top performers. Communication skills are the foundation for their success. If you don't become a great communicator then you will linger in the abyss of the average professional. I've found that communicating your knowledge and ideas to a client is critical to success.

If I were sitting next to you right now, you might ask me, "So, how will I benefit from this book if I follow your advice?" This is a great question that I definitely will answer before we begin. Based on personal research of top performers and results of clients following this program, I've seen a wide variety of value returned.

By becoming a master of client communication and following the Adviser Success Model principles you will be able to:

- build your reputation as a top performer;
- get promoted quicker;

- increase your personal income;
- increase your sales revenue;
- strengthen your profit margin;
- improve your sales win ratio;
- reduce your cost of sales;
- streamline your sales cycle;
- retain clients for life;
- sign bigger clients;
- clinch larger deals;
- close more deals;
- assemble a larger client base;
- improve client satisfaction;
- improve staff utilization;
- increase billing rates;
- boost the number of add-on sales per client;
- increase the number of referral clients.

If one or more of these benefits is a goal of yours, then you definitely need to continue reading.

Times are Tough and Getting Tougher

It's tough being a business professional today. Whether you are a business owner, consultant, sales or service professional, you run into success barriers daily. Sometimes you can become overwhelmed by the turbulent marketplace or unrealistic demands of your client. Before we discuss how you can overcome these success barriers, let's examine the challenges you are facing. Client needs have become more demanding and complex than ever before in today's competitive business environment making it tougher to become a top performer. Clients are:

- focusing on cost cutting;
- highly educated about your industry, products and services;
- highly sophisticated;
- less loyal to current providers;

- seeking long term partnerships, not short term fixes;
- require new ideas never discussed before;
- expect you to know their industry as well or better than they do;
- want you to lead their thinking;
- expect you to make a dramatic impact on their business.

Meanwhile, competitors play a role in making it tough to survive in business. These fierce, relentless competitors:

- are dissecting your business practices and;
- are entering your market quickly.

Now is the time for you to take control and eliminate these success barriers. To become a top performer in this tough business environment you need a new approach. You need to be creative and work smarter. The foundation for this new business approach is to become a master communicator. You can overcome these success barriers by following the advice and action items I describe in the following pages.

Communication Skills are Lacking

So, you don't think client communication is critical in your profession? You think you can become a top performer by ignoring this skill? Let's take a quick look at a few comments from the experts.

- Peter Drucker, a world renowned business consultant, author and speaker once said that poor communication skills are responsible for more than 60% of all organization problems.

- A *Harvard Business Review* study indicated that their readers stated the key skill sought when promoting someone in their organization was the ability to communicate well.

- A *Harvard Business Review* study revealed that business professionals spend 50% to 90% of their time communicating to others either verbally or in writing.

- Fortune magazine reported that companies are complaining about recent graduates and their lack of communication skills when entering the work force.

- The MBA program at the University of Chicago now requires students to enroll in a communication course to graduate.

- MIT is adding courses on interpersonal skills.

As you can see, the lack of good communication skills is widespread. Are you ready to turn your business or career around and start heading in the direction of a top performer?

Will This Really Help Me?

This book is intended for business owners, consultants, sales and service professionals who serve clients on a daily basis. Traditionally these are outside clients (sometimes they may be referred to as customers in your organization). Recently I've also found tremendous success implementing the art of client communication with professionals working with internal clients, that is those professionals who provide services for others within the same organization.

It doesn't matter where you fit in the above description. The tips and techniques I provide will help you become a master communicator and top performer in your profession. I will focus on the most critical communication skill areas and provide you with successfully proven techniques. This book will cover:

- Questioning – How to ask powerful, smart and insightful questions

- Listening – How to become an effective listener
- Objection Handling – How to eliminate client objections and resistance
- Preparing A Presentation – How to inspire and motivate an audience
- Delivering A Presentation – How to persuade your client to your recommendations
- Planning A Meeting – How to plan the most effective meeting
- Facilitating A Meeting – How to run the most effective meeting
- Words and Stories – How to use words and stories to get your point across
- The Written Word – How to utilize the most overlooked written communication
- Memos And Reports – How to develop powerful reports and memos
- Gatekeeper Barriers – How to get client gatekeepers to help you win
- Self Promotion – How to promote yourself to the top of your profession
- Household Name – How you can become a household name in your industry

Although there have been books published on many of these topics in the past, this book contains new approaches that focus on the critical client and business challenges you are facing today. The primary goal and objective of this program is to help you build your foundation for becoming a top performer in your profession.

My Guarantee to You

Like you, I'm a business professional looking to improve my skills on a daily basis. I want to learn from someone who has experienced the same barriers I am facing. I want to be coached by someone who can provide actionable advice, not just theoretical suggestions.

I want to learn from someone who will show me what to do, not just tell me what to do.

I guarantee this is the type of advice you will find in the following pages of this book.

Best of luck to you in your pursuit to becoming a top performer!

Adviser Success Model

**"The secret of business is knowing
something that nobody else knows."
Aristotle Onassis**

In today's fast paced changing business world, professionals must work smarter than ever to improve their performance. What worked in the past doesn't work today. Clients are more knowledgeable and demanding. Competitors are more aggressive and cut throat. Technical mastery of your vocation will only take you as far as an "average" performer.

In today's business climate, what's it going to take for you to become a top performer in your profession?

- More clients
- Bigger clients
- More deals/sales
- Bigger deals/sales
- Quicker sales cycles
- Higher win ratios
- Longer client retention
- More sales from current clients
- More add-on sales
- Improved client satisfaction

Most likely, you will need all the above.

We will now reveal the secret for becoming a top performer in your profession in the brand new, never seen before, success model that I have developed called the "Adviser Success Model".

A Recipe for Success

Three years ago I began a quest to uncover how "the best of the best" get to the top 1% of their profession. The business world is dramatically different today compared to a decade ago. The distance separating average performers to top performers is dramatically wider. What once was a gap the size of the Ohio River is now the Grand Canyon. So, the question became, "What are top performers doing differently?"

After working with top performers in the field and talking with their clients, I was able to uncover their recipes for success. Quite simply, they don't follow a popular sales process you would find in a book or seminar. They don't focus on developing additional features for their products and services. They follow a simple framework that is based on helping clients be successful. Basically, the recipe is a list of proven concepts and ideas on "what to do" to exceed client expectations. This strategy helps catapult professionals to the top of their profession.

The framework for this successful model contains four steps: Prepare, Understand, Deliver, and Nurture. The focus of each step is directly linked to the client and the value you deliver.

Figure 2.1

The amazing thing about this success model, is that it works across all professions and industries. The model is successful for any professional who must work directly with a client in either a sales or service capacity. It works equally well for both internal and external clients.

This model is not a system process where you must complete each element in a specific order. The Adviser Success Model is a framework of guidelines and actions that help you focus on the client's needs, expectations and the value you can deliver. Based on your strengths, weaknesses and goals, you decide where to focus your time. The Adviser Success Model is your recipe for becoming a top performer.

Let's take a quick look at the four steps in the Adviser Success Model.

Prepare
The first step involves "preparation". In order to achieve success as a top performer, you must do your homework before meeting the prospective client. You must learn how business and strategic planning will help you focus on the right solutions and target the right clients. Part of the preparation process is to master business communication skills. Articulating clearly to the customer is a sign of true professionalism and will reassure the potential client that you mean serious business. Taking time to acquire an in-depth understanding of the client's business and industry and finally, understanding your unique value position compared to everyone else in your industry will solidly prepare you to achieve success.

Understand
The second step focuses on completely understanding the client's needs and expectations before you discuss products and solutions. Learn how to introduce your unique value position to gain the attention of your target client. Uncover all client survival challenges and priorities by digging deep into current trouble areas and visualizing the perfect solution. Determine what success barriers

you may encounter. Understand what criteria you must meet for a solution to be successful. Last, you decide if it is in everybody's best interest for you to walk away from the opportunity.

Deliver

The third step contains the necessary elements for delivering an ultimate solution exceeding client expectations. Your solution must be focused on delivering client value which increases revenue or reduces costs. Performance metrics must be measurable and available for visibility in a scorecard. When delivering your solution recommendations, your message needs to be inspiring and persuasive. At this point, a "go" decision to move forward should be nearly automatic.

Nurture

The forth step focuses on gaining the client's trust and becoming their lifelong adviser. You will earn trust by over delivering on results. You will strengthen your client relationship by treating clients as a business partner. A client account strategy will become your strategic planning tool that both you and your client will use as a living success roadmap. And finally, once you deliver a solution, you will monitor the solution value metrics and you will take appropriate action if needed.

If you are ready to become a top performer in your industry, consider looking deeper into the Adviser Success Model. This will become your recipe for success.

Adviser Success Model Quick Reference

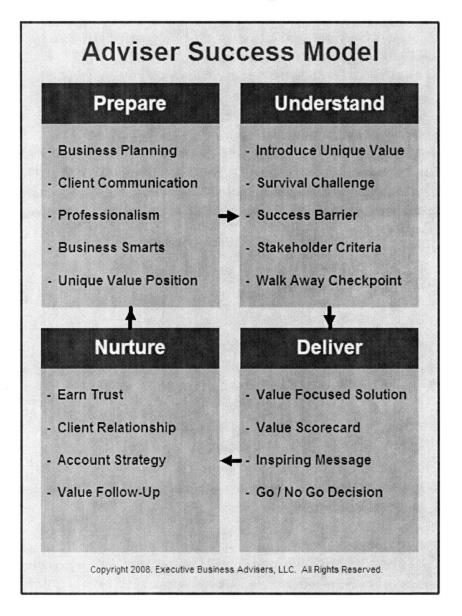

Figure 2.2

Client Communication – Building Your Foundation

Undeniably, one of the most important skills for top performers to master are communication skills. For this reason, client communication is one of the first elements we discuss in the Adviser Success Model – Prepare section. So, why do most professional training programs and books either ignore or graze over this topic? Many believe that technical and process knowledge is more important to their business. Others see communication skills as something you can easily learn on the job. When talking with top performers, you will find the opposite is true. After business planning, client communication is the skill set that allows them to maximize sales revenue, customer satisfaction and client retention.

Client Communication

- Questioning

- Listening

- Speaking

- Written Word

- Promotion

Figure 2.3

Let's review the five client communication skills covered in the Adviser Success Model.

Questioning

To solve a difficult challenge you must ask the right questions. Asking simple yes/no questions is not sufficient to become a top performer. First, you need to understand the questions that you must avoid. Next you need to learn how to ask powerful smart questions for gathering key information. The type of questions you ask, how you ask them and when you ask them will dramatically change how your client perceives you. Smart questions lead to smart answers, which in return leads you to providing the best solution for your client.

Listening

To truly understand, you can't just listen to what people are saying. You must effectively listen. Most professionals effectively listen only 25% of the time. Unfortunately, effective listening is a very difficult skill to master. Top performers spend a good portion of their time mastering the 11 techniques of an effective listener. By talking less and listening effectively, top performers can solve problems quicker, promote new business discussion, open up the client's mind to new ideas and earn the client's lifelong trust.

Speaking

The key to speaking is quality, not quantity. Most professionals talk too much. Remember that sometimes less is more. Top performers have learned that speaking less is more productive when you master the speaking skills for different situations. They learn how to eliminate objections and resistance before they happen. When involved in public speaking it is important for you to overcome the fear of speaking in front of groups no matter how large or small. It is also important to become a master meeting planner and facilitator. Top performers learn the unique skills needed when talking with different clients, gatekeepers and assistants.

Written Word

In today's world of email, texting and IMing we have forgotten the fine art of great business communication. Top performers focus on quality written communication. They use the most effective words and stories based on the client's profile and personality. They write memos and business documents that make an impact and persuade their clients. Top Performers also find tremendous benefit in the lost art of keeping a business journal and sending out hand written thank you notes.

Promotion

Finally, when you tie together questioning, listening, speaking and the written word you have all the skills to promote yourself to the top. Top performers learn how to tie these skills together into a self promotion tool package that attract clients quickly and earn them top dollar for the products and services they provide.

The following chapters provide you with a step-by-step guide for the Client Communication section of the Adviser Success Model. For more information on the entire success model, please contact Executive Business Advisers at www.executivebusinessadvisers. com or Dennis Sommer at www.dennissommer.com.

My Top Book Recommendations

If you would like to research this topic in more detail, I highly recommend the following books.

- The 4-Hour Workweek: Escape 9-5, Live Anywhere, and Join the New Rich, by Timothy Ferriss, ISBN-13: 978-0307353139

- Getting Things Done: The Art of Stress-Free Productivity, by David Allen, ISBN-13: 978-0142000281

- The Tipping Point: How Little Things Can Make a Big Difference, by Malcolm Gladwell, ISBN-13: 978-0316346627

1. Gaining True Insight Through Questions

Have you ever had trouble getting someone to open up? You sit there, ask how you can help, and spend the next 30 minutes in silence. Asking the right questions encourages people to become more willing to open up their imagination, stimulates the search for information, provides key pieces of data that are critical for solving their challenges and differentiates you from your competitors. Asking the right questions is not a fad. This is a powerful age old technique that has been lost by many, but used effectively by top performers.

In this chapter you will learn:
- □ 5 types of questions you must avoid
- □ How to develop powerful (smart) questions
- □ 50 powerful sample questions
- □ 5 questioning tips delivering maximum results

Yes, There Are Dumb Questions

All our lives we have been told "there are no dumb questions." We heard it from our parents, teachers, trainers and bosses. I've been witness to hundreds of dumb questions throughout my career and life. How about you?

You might be a business owner, consultant, sales or service professional, but you're also someone's client. Therefore, like myself, you've been in your client's shoes. Have you ever been asked a question that totally turned you off to what they were proposing or one that made you ask the person to leave your office? I'm sure you could share many stories about how a sales person lost business because they asked the wrong question.

At the top of my "dumbest questions ever" list is; "Why would you want to do that?" I've lost count of the number of times someone has posed that question. I find this question insulting and it places a client on the defensive. A person asking me this will never get my business. Would you purchase a product or service from someone asking this? Better yet, do you ask this type of question when you're with a client?

If you want to be the top performer in your profession, make sure you are ask "smart" questions. What are smart questions? These are prompts that motivate people to open up. They produce thought, new ideas, entice the imagination and encourage further discussion. Smart questions stimulate the thirst for more information. When you ask smart questions, you create forward momentum that will deliver positive results for both you and your client.

Asking smart questions is not a fad or new trend that will change the world. This is an age-old lesson that has passed from one top performer to another. The type of question you ask, how you ask it and when you ask it will dramatically change how clients perceive you. Smart questions lead to smart answers, which in return, helps you provide the best solution for your clients.

Questions To Avoid

Before we examine the smart powerful questions used by top performers, let's first review questions to avoid. You are permitted to use the types of questions in this section with a client in some circumstances. However, they do not produce the results expected by top performers.

1. Questions Starting With "Why"

You should avoid "Why" questions completely. From a client's perspective, starting a question with "why" sounds confrontational and insulting. The question immediately puts your client on the defensive and he or she may become less willing to provide quality answers going forward. Let's take a look at a few standard "why" questions:

- Why is price part of your decision process?
- Why do you feel that way?
- Why do you buy from that vendor?

After hearing these questions, do you feel defensive? Most likely you do, just like your clients. Now, these are valid questions. If you want the best answers, just replace "why" with something like "How" or "What" and rephrase the question. For example, instead of "Why is price part of your decision process?", ask "What role does price have in your decision?" This prompts the customer to offer a response. The next time you ask a client questions, keep "why" out of the discussion.

2. Blunt Questions

Blunt questions are straight-forward, direct, and to the point. Your client will have no trouble understanding what type of answer you want. Let's take a look at some examples:

- Do you have the authority to sign this contract?
- Do you want this to succeed?
- Is price important to you?

Unfortunately, many clients find blunt questions offensive or threatening. To obtain the best results, try softening this question using the techniques we describe in the Powerful (Smart) Questions section of this chapter.

3. Leading Questions

Leading questions tend to suggest the answer you desire. They are biased questions that try to elicit a specific response. For example:

- Price is important to you, isn't it?
- You do like this product, don't you?

How do these questions make you feel? If you are like most clients, you feel cornered and manipulated. These questions do not help you elicit quality information. They only alienate you from you client.

4. General Questions

In most sales and soft skill seminars you have been trained to start your client sessions with general non threatening questions leading to more specific questions. The theory is, you built up rapport and ease the client into more detail questions. For example, you might start a session with the following:

- How long have you been with the organization?
- Tell me about your company?
- What trends do you see in your industry?
- Who are your customers?
- Who is your competition?

The trouble with this line of questioning is clients expect you to already know the answers. As a top performer in your profession, you should have done your homework and already understand who the client is, what they do and how they are performing. Going in with these softball questions makes you look like a rookie on his first client call. If you don't already have the answers to these general questions, cancel your client meeting.

5. Closed-Ended Questions

A closed-ended question is structured in a way that produces a short specific response. Usually the response is "yes" or "no". Sometimes the answer is one sentence. A closed-ended question does not allow for the client to expand on their answer. You will rarely uncover the root cause of an issue or understand their true needs because the question is too confining. This is not to say they should never be used. Closed-ended questions are best used as a follow-up question when you need clarification or confirmation. They are also useful when you need a specific piece of information like a quantity, time or dollar value.

Most closed-ended questions begin with words like:
- Are you
- Do you
- How many
- How much
- When
- Where
- Which
- Who
- Will you

Let's take a look at a few closed-ended questions.
- Are you having issues?
- Which product do you prefer?
- Do you like your current product?

Now that you know what to avoid, let's take a look at how you can create powerful (smart) questions that get results.

Powerful (Smart) Questions
for Every Situation

Everyone knows that to solve a difficult challenge you must ask the right questions. However, simple yes/no type questions will only lead your client down the path you choose. Arming yourself with powerful open ended questions is a vital tool used by top performers for gathering key information that will help them deliver the best possible solution. In this section we will list some of the powerful questions that top performers use. Become familiar with these and start adding more specific questions about your industry and solutions.

Open-Indirect Questions

An "Open-Indirect" question is the cornerstone of the powerful smart question. This type of question encourages the client to elaborate and provide a lengthy response. The advantage is the client will volunteer additional information and describe their position thoroughly. They will become deeply involved in the solution. The added advantage is your client will not feel threatened or cornered. Emotionally, they will open up fully. Typically, an "Open-Indirect" question will begin with "How", "What", or "Tell me". Lets' take a look at a few examples:

- What are your main concerns in selecting a solution?
- How do you feel about moving to a new system?
- What type of investment are you willing to make in a solution?
- Tell me more about your inventory shrink challenges?

Wow! See what I mean? This type of question is powerful. You can take any question and transform it into a powerful smart question that gets results.

Now that you understand how to structure the question, let's take a look at a few more examples. We have categorized them into situation scenarios. When you are planning your next client meeting, use this list of examples for inspiration.

Understanding Challenges and Needs
- What would your primary use be for this type solution?
- What would you most like to change about your current situation?

- What are your expectations?
- What are your top 10 challenges you are facing?
- What are your top priorities?
- What challenges does that create for you?
- What challenges has that created for you in the past?
- What has prompted your organization to look into this type of solution?
- What is the biggest challenge you are facing today?
- What is working really well today?
- What other challenges are important to you?
- What other items should we discuss further?
- What would the perfect solution look like?
- What would you like to see accomplished?
- What would you like to see improved?
- How did you determine your needs and requirements?
- How do you measure that?
- How does that work now?
- What concerns do you have?
- What do you attribute that to?
- What other problems does that create for you?
- What areas would you improve on?
- If your budget was of no concern, what would you like this solution to look like?
- In a perfect world, what would a business partner be doing for you?

Understanding Value
- What is the result if you do nothing?
- What would it mean to you if you could improve your present situation?
- What are your expected outcomes from a solution?
- What type of investment are your willing to make in this solution?
- How does that impact your business?
- What is the impact on your customers?

Clarification Questions
- Can you help me understand this better?
- Can you tell me more?
- What am I missing?
- What are your thoughts?
- What do you think should happen next?
- What do you think we should do?
- What does that mean?
- Suppose you could…, what would that enable you to do?

Qualification Questions
- What concerns do you have?
- What is the investment budget approved for this solution?
- What could happen to make this a lower priority?
- What do you see as the next steps?
- What has changed since we last discussed this?
- What is your timeframe for implementing a solution?
- What is your timeframe for purchasing a solution?
- What is your timeframe for starting this project?
- What resources are you going to dedicate to this?
- What areas of the company are also affected by this decision?
- How does your decision process work?
- What would you like to see happen here?

Questioning Tips That Get Results

Tip 1: Prepare In Advance
Of course, every client meeting is unique. A standard list of questions pulled out of your folder will not be effective. To get the most out of your questions, you need to sit and plan what questions to ask. These unique, client specific questions should be focused on your meeting goals. For example, "To better understand your current challenges and expectations". By carefully planning the questions to ask, you will be able to cover everything you need to achieve your goal.

Tip 2: Rehearse Before Your Meeting

Reading from a list of questions makes you look unprepared. Review your list of questions to get a general feel for how you will be conducting your meeting. Don't memorize every question. This will sound canned and limit the flow of conversation. As your discussion progresses, you can interject questions at the appropriate time. Keep your list close and use it as a guide if you become stuck on where to take the conversation next.

Tip 3: Have A Discussion, Not An Interrogation

Rattling off questions is a good way to turn off your client and get you excused early. An endless stream of questions is an interrogation not a discussion. Using the "Open-Indirect" questions above will help create a discussion. Asking the client to expand on their answer will keep the discussion moving and provide more in-depth detail.

Tip 4: Ask Permission First

The best way to start this type of discussion is by asking, "Do you mind if I ask you a few questions?" The question is polite and respectful and a great way to start a conversation. Your client will most likely say, "Sure, what would you like to ask?".

Now, at this point in my seminars there is usually one person who stands up and says, "I thought we are supposed to avoid closed-ended questions like this?" Yes, that is true. This is one of the exceptions where you are looking for a short answer to gain permission to continue.

Tip 5: Shut Up And Listen

Your client can't answer your questions if you keep talking. You'll never hear their answer. Look them in the eyes, ask your questions, then zip your lip. Listen to their response and absorb every word they say. This tip is so important; we have even dedicated a full chapter to it.

Smart questioning is a valuable tool in the business world. The better you become at asking questions, the easier it will be for you to become the top performer in your profession.

My Top Book Recommendations

If you would like to research this topic in more detail, I highly recommend the following books.

- Leading with Questions: How Leaders Find the Right Solutions By Knowing What To Ask, by Michael J. Marquardt, ISBN-13: 978-0787977467

- How to Ask Great Questions: Guide Your Group to Discovery With These Proven Techniques, by Karen Lee-Thorp, ISBN-13: 978-1576830789

- Questions That Work: How to Ask Questions That Will Help You Succeed in Any Business Situation, by Andrew Finlayson, ISBN-13: 978-0814473290

What you will learn next?

In the next chapter we focus on how you can solve problems quicker, understand a client's needs better and earn their trust and respect by becoming an effective listener.

2. How Can You Truly Understand if You Don't Listen

Many professionals are so involved in what they have to say, they end up controlling the entire conversation. Unfortunately, this is the last thing you want to do. Top performers make the time count by listening attentively to their client's needs and concerns. Keener listening skills will help you solve problems more quickly, understand a client's needs better and earn their trust and respect. Today we will transform you from a "talker" to a "listener".

In this chapter you will learn:
- □   5 key benefits when you talk less and listen more
- □   11 listening barriers you must avoid
- □   11 tips and techniques for becoming an effective listener
- □   36 dos and don'ts of top performers

Shut Up and Listen

I was shocked and amazed! John, a Senior Account Manager for a large software technology company randomly called a well known financial services firm to pitch his product. Amazingly, the firm invited John to personally come in and talk with their executive committee about a new strategic project. At this meeting, all John had to do was listen to the requirements to satisfy their technology needs.

But no, John could not keep his mouth shut. Every step of the way he interrupted his client to interject his solution features, capabilities and personal thoughts on what the client should do. You could see in the client's expression that John was not there to understand the client's challenges. John was only interested in pitching his solution. I was sure after thirty minutes the client would ask John to leave. But no, the client listened respectfully and thanked John for coming in. Two weeks later we learned the client selected an inferior solution with another company. John lost a $1 million contract that should have been an easy sell.

Have you witnessed this before? Have you done this yourself at least once in your career?

In the previous chapter "Gaining True Insight through Questions" you learned the importance and value of great questions. The process of asking powerful smart (Open Indirect) questions will produce superior answers from your clients. Just as important, when your client is responding to your questions, you need to effectively listen to their answers. In a study by Dr. Ralph Nichol's, he found that we devote 40% of our day listening. His tests also revealed that out of the 40% time spent listening, only 25% was effective listening. Therefore, in a 60 minute discussion, on average a person listens for 24 minutes. Out of that 24 minutes, you only effectively listen for 6 minutes. For 18 minutes you do not hear what is being said. If you are not hearing 75% of what your client says, you will not be able to provide them with a solution that can overcome their challenges and meet their goals.

Average 60 Minute Discussion

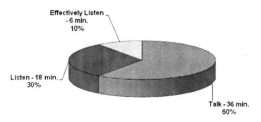

Figure 4.1

What is the definition of listening? If you look at the Merriam-Webster Dictionary, you will find the following definition for "Listening": 1) to pay attention to sound 2) to hear something with thoughtful attention: give consideration 3) to be alert to catch an expected sound.

Clients of top performers (those in the top 1% of their industry) have repeatedly stated that just listening isn't enough. Top performers effectively listen and rarely do the talking. The definition of effective listening, from the client's perspective, would look something like this:

"An effective listener is someone who refrains from talking too much and making judgments about others. They place themselves in the client's shoes to see things from their perspective. They are attentive to both verbal and non-verbal communication. They are empathetic to the client's feelings and thoughts over their own. An effective listener shows verbal and non- verbal signs that they are truly listening. The overall focus is to understand the client's challenges, needs, wants and goals-- to truly understand."

At this point, I usually get two questions. 1) How much listening should we do? 2) How can I improve my listening skills? We will address question one now and question two later in this chapter.

When observing top performers, I have found that the breakdown looks something like this: A top performer will talk around 20% of the time, usually asking powerful smart questions. They then spend 80% of the conversation effectively listening to the client. This means, in a 60 minute conversation a top performer is asking questions for 12 minutes and effectively listening for 48 minutes. Think about this impact. An average listener only effectively listens for 6 minutes vs. a top performer who effectively listens for 48 minutes.

Top Performer - 60 Minute Discussion

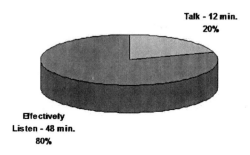

Figure 4.2

Now, let's examine the benefits you can achieve when listening like a top performer and how you can improve your skills today.

Many Benefits When You Truly Listen

There are plenty of reasons to talk less and listen more. Those who have the gift of gab or believe that power and persuasion are directly related to the amount of time they talk are missing out on huge rewards. Those who sell more, attract clients forever, or earn the largest fees are the ones who reap the rewards of listening effectively.

Some of the huge rewards you will gain after improving your listening skills include:

1. Solving Problems Quicker

When a client is able to talk through a challenge he or she will clarify his or her thinking about the problem, expected results and actions that may overcome the challenge. By asking the right questions and letting your client talk through his or her answers, he or she may solve the problem themselves. You become their catalyst for results.

2. Promoting Further Discussion

Communication between you and a client is essential for the success of both parties. Communication can break down quickly if one of the parties is not listening effectively. Listening helps you to promote communication that will lead to further business discussions.

3. Opening the Mind To New Ideas

When you listen effectively, you try to understand the client's true feelings and needs. You are putting yourself in their shoes. This process keeps your mind active and involved in the discussion resulting in new creative ideas that will help your client.

4. Reducing Emotions

Listening more gives your client the opportunity to voice their complaints and troubles. They are able to release their hostilities and tensions and thus, clear the air. Once the client releases emotion he or she will be more open to explore his or her challenges and your recommendations.

5. Earning Respect

When a client feels that you are truly interested in their well being they will cooperate with you unconditionally. This leads to respecting you as a person and professional.

Why Listening is Difficult to Master

Listening sounds like it should be the easiest thing for us to do. We have been listening to sounds and words from the day we were born. Many people don't see listening as an issue and would rather spend their time and money on something else. Unfortunately, there are many barriers that obstruct effective listening. Yes, we may hear the sounds, but are we listening effectively? As the study above demonstrated, the average person listens effectively only 25% of the time. Then why is effective listening so difficult to master?

Let's take a look at the barriers you face when listening.

1. Cultural Perception
We are taught that the speaker represents power and authority. We perceive people who speak a great deal during meetings, regardless of what they say, as having the qualities of an expert. This cultural perception leads to the negative perception that listening is a passive weak act.

2. Daydreaming
It's more enjoyable to think about the white sand beaches, surf and sunshine of your last vacation.

3. External Interference
You are distracted by the sights and sounds around you. You are looking out the window at the cruising sail boats in the inner harbor. You are trying to hear the side conversation of two VP's sitting next to you.

4. Hearing Only Words
You don't pick up the non-verbal responses from the client. You are only listening to their words.

5. Impatient
There is a time gap between speaking and listening that makes you impatient. We speak an average of 225 words per minute but our brains can digest and analyze around 400 words per minute. This discrepancy makes us impatient and sometimes leads us to finish a client's sentence or interject our thoughts before they have finished.

6. Internal Interference
You're thinking about your next meeting, your grocery shopping list or what to buy your spouse for his or her birthday tomorrow.

7. Job Is To Talk
As an expert in your industry you are trained to talk about your expertise and knowledge. You most likely exert energy working on your sales pitch or presentation. So, your energy is channeled into telling your story with very little time to focus on listening.

8. Know It All
You alone already have all the answers. You are the expert in your field. You just need the client to stop talking so you can jump in and gain control of the discussion.

9. Overloaded
You have received too much information from the client. Your mind is full and you can't think.

10. Time Crunch
You feel rushed due to time pressure. The discussion is only scheduled for one hour. You don't have enough time to demonstrate your knowledge and expertise.

11. You're Lost
The discussion is filled with technical jargon that is way over your head. You're in the fog and can't see where this discussion has been or where it is going. All you can think about is "What are they talking about?"

Many, if not all of these interfere with your ability to be an effective listener. Now that we have identified our barriers, let's explore how we can overcome them.

How to Become an Effective Listener

Before reading this chapter did you ever think you might have a listening problem or, that your listening skills might be holding you back from becoming a top performer? Many professionals like you have approached me after my seminars and say they thought they were good listeners but now realize they are poor listeners. This realization is not surprising since listening skill development is not covered well, if at all, in our professional training. Add to that the barriers we discussed previously and you can understand that effective listening can be a challenge-- but a challenge that we can overcome by mastering a few effective listening tips and techniques.

The following tips and techniques will help you become an effective listener.

1. Ask for clarification.
Effective listening implies you understand what people say. When you're unsure about something, ask for clarification. You might say "Can you tell me more about…" or "What does it mean when you say…" Asking for clarification demonstrates that you care about the client and are paying attention to what they are saying. It will also help you better understand the client's needs so you can offer them the best solution.

2. Avoid distractions.
We do not hold most of our client discussions in a sound proof, windowless, clutter free room. There are many visual and audible distractions that pull us away from effectively listening to our client. It's very easy to lose focus when a side conversation starts next to you or you are distracted when you look out the window on a bright sunny spring day and see birds floating carefree in the sky. To avoid these distractions, keep your eyes and ears focused directly at the client. Position your body away from the distractions, if possible. This will help you focus on the client, which also shows you have the client's full attention.

3. Don't interrupt your client.

Many professionals are so excited to make their point they jump in with their solution before the client can complete a thought or sentence. Interrupting a client is not only annoying and rude, it doesn't give him or her the opportunity to fully answer the question or describe his or her situation. Be patient. Allow your client ample time to answer a question or explain a situation. Do not speak until you are fully confident that he or she has completed his or her thought.

4. Focus on one topic at a time.

Since the average person speaks 225 words a minute and your mind can process 400 words per minute, you can quickly lose focus. You need to consciously focus on the topic of discussion, the words and the non-verbal signs or cues. Don't let you mind wonder off.

5. Listen with your gut.

Effective listening is a whole body experience. You may hear the words and see the non-verbal signs or cues, however sometimes your gut feelings are a good indicator for what you are hearing and seeing. What are you feeling when talking with your client? If you are sensing something is wrong and doesn't match what he or she is saying, ask for clarification or how he or she feels about XYZ. Sometimes the feeling behind the message is the real message.

6. Remove unnerving ticks.

Finger drumming, toe tapping, pen tapping, foot stomping and excessive leg movement are signs that you are not interested in what is being said. These are considered nervous habits and limit your ability to listen. If you suffer from nerves when interacting with clients, it is helpful to practice relaxation techniques, especially before you enter a meeting situation. A calm body will enhance your ability to listen.

7. Restate a summary of what you have heard.

Throughout your conversation, summarize what your client has said. For example, "So, your main challenge today is ..." Restating what your client said demonstrates that you are truly listening and understand what he or she is saying. When you actively summarize, you will focus more on the client and improve your listening abilities.

8. Take bullet point notes.
Have you ever tried to remember the details of a complex thirty minute discussion without having notes? After thirty minutes of discussion, were you truly listening to the client or thinking back to what he or she said ten minutes ago? Note taking demonstrates to your client that his or her words are very important to you. It also helps you organize information in a way that will help you listen more effectively and provide a better solution. Taking notes does not mean you copy down every single word. By doing this you will concentrate more on writing the words than truly listening to the content. Develop your own shorthand or take notes in bullet point format. Note the key points in less than five words.

9. Use silence as a tool.
Silence can be unnerving and intimidating which is why so many professionals avoid it. After asking a question, keep silent while your client thinks about his or her response. Don't jump in with a rephrased question because you think he or she didn't understand the first question. Give him or her time to think about the answer and give the response. When the client has finished talking, nod your head and silently count to five before you speak. This silence may draw out more information, or at worst, confirm he or she has completed his or her thought on that topic.

10. Use your body language.
Does your body language demonstrate you are listening to the client? Subconsciously are you resisting what he or she is saying – folding your arms or pulling away? There are many other non-verbal signals that result from not listening. Improving your body language enhances your ability to listen effectively. Try leaning forward, keep your arms open and nod. This type of body language demonstrates to your client that you are actively engaged in the discussion.

11. Watch for non-verbal signals/cues.

While listening to the spoken word you also need to observe non-verbal signals/cues. Does your client avoid eye contact meaning he or she is not comfortable discussing the topic? Are the client's arms folded tight indicating he or she might be withholding information? Is the client displaying uninterested signals such as nervous finger drumming to indicate that you are talking too much? Watch for all non-verbal signals when you engage with a client in order to better understand what the client is really saying.

Do's and Don'ts of Top Performers

You have just learned that most professionals have poor listening skills, why this occurs and how to overcome it. Let's examine a final list of what top performers do, or don't do, that make them such effective listeners.

Top Performers Don't:
- ask closed-ended (yes/no type) questions;
- assume they already know what the client is going to say, even before he or she says it;
- daydream while the client is speaking;
- form a response in their head while the client is speaking;
- give opinions before they hear the client's;
- give the appearance of listening when they really are not;
- interrupt the client while he or she is talking;
- judge a client based on his or her personality, looks or background;
- jump to conclusions or make judgments before you collect all the facts;
- respond with a solution before the client has fully described his or her challenge;
- take calls, respond to text messages or emails during the discussion.

Top Performers Do:

- acknowledge the client with nodding, smiling and verbal queues like yes, hmm, oh?;
- ask for clarification of technical jargon that they are not familiar with;
- keep themselves aware of the story behind the discussion;
- concentrate on the client's message if they don't agree or are not interested;
- eliminate internal/personal distractions;
- remove outside distractions;
- empathize with the client;
- give undivided attention to the client, making it seem like he or she are the only thing that matters;
- identify assumptions that are implied but not expressed;
- keep digging for more details;
- engage the client by asking powerful, smart, open in-direct questions;
- leave their ego at home;
- allow the client get negative emotions off their chest, blow off steam
- permit the client to tell his or her story in his or her words or way;
- make eye contact while the client is talking;
- observe the non-verbal emotions;
- analyze what is different in content, not what's familiar
- paraphrase what they believe the client is feeling
- place themselves in the client's shoes;
- probe continuously for clarification of discussion points;
- remain in control of excessive body movement like fidgeting, tapping feet, shaking legs or playing with a pen;
- summarize what the client said using their own words;
- take every discussion seriously;
- think about how the person will react to what they say;
- Center words and actions around "How can I help you?"

My Top Book Recommendations

If you would like to research this topic in more detail, I highly recommend the following books.

- Listening: The Forgotten Skill: A Self-Teaching Guide, by Madelyn Burley-Allen, ISBN-13: 978-0471015871

- Are You Really Listening?: Keys to Successful Communication, by Paul J., Ph.D. Donoghue, Mary E. Siegel, ISBN-13: 978-1893732889
- Listen Up!: How to Communicate Effectively at Work, by Eunice Lemay, Jane Schwamberger, ISBN-13: 978-0978805852

What will you learn next?

In the next chapter we focus on how you can improve customer satisfaction, increase sales and quickly gain client support by eliminating objections before they happen.

3. Eliminate Client Objections and Resistance

You're not experienced enough in the industry. Your company is too small. I like what I'm using today. Your prices are too high. Have you heard any of these statements in the past week? The list of objections you hear on a daily basis is long and they are most likely stopping you from becoming a top performer. Eliminating objections will allow you to quickly gain client support for your ideas and recommendations. It will also lead to higher customer satisfaction and increase your success rate.

In this chapter you will learn:
- How to prepare yourself for 27 objection signals
- 6 techniques that eliminate 95% of client objections
- 3 steps to turn your weaknesses into strengths
- The best techniques for handling price objections
- 3 bonus tips and techniques from top performers

Feeling the Objection Pain

Dwayne, the new VP of Sales for a major technology company had just finished his weekly sales status meeting when we met for lunch. After ordering our drinks and discussing the exciting basketball game that went into double overtime the previous night, I asked a simple open ended question – "So, how is your sales organization doing this year?" Little did I know, the answer to this one simple question would last three hours and many drinks later.

Dwayne talked about how his industry is growing at 33%, the smaller companies his business has acquired, the new products released in the past year and how the company spent millions of dollars training his sale force. Hey, these are the reasons why he joined the company in the first place. So, after six months on the job why is he so miserable? Sales are down, client retention is declining, the sales cycle is 21% longer than normal and the signed deals average 18% less than prior years. Wow! This is the nightmare scenario that every sales manager and business executive wants to avoid.

During our lunch, one probing question started us down the path to finding the primary root cause of Dwayne's problem. The question was "During your – Deal/No Deal Lessons Learned Reviews – what are you hearing?" Dwayne started listing reason after reason. The company is too big now, price is too high, products are too new, quality is poor, and on and on. We both quickly came to the conclusion that these simple objections were causing the company's major down turn.

I asked Dwayne why all the sudden in the last year they were getting these objections? His short statement said it all, "Our sales training focuses on creating objections because they are a signal that the client is interested in buying. The more objections you get from the client, the easier it will be to get the deal." I almost choked on my breadstick with that statement. Once again, here is an example of a company sucked into the misleading myths of standard sales training.

The "Real Truth" is, when you hear an objection from a client, it usually means you have not qualified the client well, communicated your value correctly, differentiated yourself from competitors, or how your product or service will drive business results.

Let's explore this topic of objections and resistance in more detail. Also, we will review how you can jump start your sales and business performance by eliminating all objections and resistance before they happen.

Understanding Objection Signals

During discussions with clients, you will receive signals (verbal and non- verbal) on what concerns them, what they are thinking and how they are feeling. These signals will be in the form of questions they ask, the tone of their voice, the pace of their speech, the inflection made, and non- verbal body language. As a top performer you need to be aware of these signals and be prepared to respond.

Let's look at the most common examples of objection and resistance signals you must be prepared for:

1. I am just collecting data to analyze.
2. I am loyal to your competitor.
3. I am too busy to deal with this now.
4. I don't have the authority to approve this.
5. I had a bad experience with your company in the past.
6. I have no immediate need.
7. I have no money for this.
8. I have other priorities.
9. I just don't want to work with your company.
10. I want to wait and see what happens.
11. You have not shown me how this will solve my problem.
12. Your company is financially unstable.
13. Your company is too big.
14. Your company is too small.
15. Your company reputation is horrible.

16. Your product/service doesn't offer a total solution.
17. Your product/service has too many flaws.
18. Your product/service is not quality based.
19. Your product/service is too new.
20. Your product/service is too old.
21. Your product/service is too risky.
22. Your product/service is unproven.
23. Your product/service price is too high.
24. Your product/service price is too low.
25. Your product/service takes too long to implement.
26. Your product/service will not be available when I need it.
27. Your terms are not acceptable.

This list of objections and many more linger in the minds of business executives whenever they are making decisions to buy from you. Your goal as the top performer is too eliminate these objections before they happen. If you do, you will reap the rewards of higher sales, larger deals and improved client satisfaction and retention.

Eliminate 95% of the Objections Before They Happen

Most client objections and resistance are not initiated by them, they are initiated by you. Traditional training workshops have told you to focus on your company, capabilities and features. These key points are the main cause for most of the objections and resistance you encounter when dealing with a client. These factors are also the main reasons why your sales closure rate is probably around 25%.

Here is a simple example of a typical conversation that ends with an objection:

Client:	I would like an inventory control system for my small business.
You:	What type of system are you looking for?
Client:	I want something that will keep accurate counts and increase picking times.
You:	We have just what you need. Our new IC product will provide you with inventory control, picking, shipping and more than 256 advanced features, 50 template reports and additional capabilities that will handle time and labor control. This product is the best in the market and can be up and running for only $200,000.
Client:	Client considers his need versus the proposed solution.
Client:	The solution is not worth it. I'll live with what I have.

The client objection has just killed the deal. What happened? We have been trained to follow a simple pattern that supposedly will clinch quickly the most deals for us, at higher revenues. We are taught the following technique which causes most of our client objections.

1. Understand need.
2. Determine which product/service will fill that need.
3. Describe your product/service capabilities, features and advantages.
4. Ask for the sale.

Result – Objection, resistance and lost clients.

To eliminate objections and resistance, you need to change your technique to focus more on the client's challenges, priorities, expectations, and solution value. Is the client's perceived need valid? Will any product or service solve the true problem or just the symptom? By following the value based technique below you can prevent any objection or resistance from coming into play during your discussions.

1. Understand the Challenges

What are all the business issues, problems and challenges that the client is having today or expects in the future? You need to dig deeper into *why* you are there. For example, what challenges is the company facing that would initiate the decision to look for a new inventory control system? You need to uncover and list all the issues, problems and challenges. For example, one issue might be that lost inventory has increased this year. Once you are able to identify and list all the challenges, ask the client to prioritize them, with number one as the most important. This prioritized list provides you with the client's perceived list of most important challenges. You can now continue to address their top priorities first.

2. Gather Examples

How do we know that there really is a problem? You need to ask for examples of data or scenarios that confirm the size of the problem. This data should include tangible numbers, percents and time. The examples could include data involving financials, quality, productivity and quantity. For example, lost inventory has increased 13% this year costing us an additional $265,000.

3. Define Expectations

What would the perfect solution look like? The answer to this simple question will define the ultimate solution that the client expects. This is not the description of a product or service, but how the business would operate differently. For example, I would like keep tighter control of inventory, keeping lost inventory below 2%. Next, you need to quantify the value this perfect solution would bring to the business. You might ask, "What would be the financial impact on your company by keeping lost inventory at or below 2%". An example response could be, "At 2% we would reduce lost inventory costs by $965,000.

For every challenge defined in step one, you should go through the prioritized list and gather examples and expectations. Once compiled, you will now have a complete inventory of the root causes, examples that prove there is a problem, what the solution should look like, and how these challenges are impacting the business.

4. Understand Success Barriers

This may be the most overlooked step in selling or client relations today. To overcome objections and resistance, you need to understand what barriers you may face. What are the potential traps or road blocks that you must consider before you can develop an approved solution and a decision to move forward.

Barriers may include:
- Operations – Other business areas affected by the challenges and solutions.
- Organization – Business strategies, goals and objectives affected by a solution.
- The Past – What has stopped them from solving this challenge in the past?
- Timing – What are the expected start and completion dates?
- Staffing – Who will be doing the work?
- Investment – What investment are you willing to make to solve your challenges?

Pose questions to the client addressing the above barriers. When you identify success barriers, discuss how you can eliminate the barrier or lesson it to the point that it would not impact the decision or success of the project. Sometimes you might find an unmovable barrier. For example, they must have a complete, full feature inventory control system installed and running smoothly in the next 45 days. The company cannot move this deadline and anything delivered after that date would not be acceptable. If you already know your solution would require a minimum of 6 months, then at this point you can walk away saving everyone from a loss/loss situation.

5. Deliver A Value Focused Solution

You are now at the final step for delivering a recommended solution that will focus on the business value you can deliver, eliminating any client objections or resistance. Using the information you collected during your discussion, you can now deliver a proposed solution that will meet the client's expectations.

Your recommended solution should include:
- Understanding The Challenges - Restatement of the key business challenges in priority order.
- Gathering Examples - Re-statement of how this is impacting the organization.
- Define Expectations - Restatement of the client's desired outcome or expectations when complete.
- Your Solution – The products and services you propose to the client that will address their challenges and deliver their expected results. Your solution will also address any success barriers you have identified in your discussions.
- Your Value Proposition – The client has already given you the key tangible data to define how this challenge is impacting his or her business. You have re-stated above in their words that these challenges are costing them X dollars and deceased productivity. The client has also stated the impact when the new expectations are met. Now you can show the client that your solution will meet or exceed their expectations, delivering $X value to their organization with and investment of $X. This solution will have a Return on Investment (ROI) of $X or X%. Your value proposition could also include other value metrics like; Internal Rate of Return, Break Even Point, Net Present Value and Payback Period.

As you can see, this technique is vastly different from what you are traditionally taught. Does it require more time to deliver? Yes, absolutely. Is it worth the time? Yes, absolutely.

Let's return to our first example of a typical conversation. The client determined that the solution was not worth it. Now, let's take another look at that simplified conversation using our value based techniques. Do you think the results might be different?

Client:	I would like an inventory control system for my small business.
You:	What issues or problems are you having today or expect to have in the future?
Client:	Lost inventory is a big problem and also…
You:	You just described 11 key issues. Can you prioritize your concerns from the most to the least important?
Client:	Sure, our number one concern is…, our second concern is…
You:	Great. Let's first discuss lost inventory in more detail. Can you show me examples of how this is affecting your business? What tangible examples of dollars, percentages, etc. have you uncovered?
Client:	Well, over the past year, lost inventory has increased 13% costing us $265,000.
You:	If you could picture the perfect solution to this problem what would it look like?
Client:	I would like to have tighter control of my inventory keeping lost inventory at or below 2% per year.
You:	What impact would that have on your business?
Client:	At 2% we would reduce lost inventory costs by $965,000.
Both:	Continue through the other 10 items
You:	Will any other business area be impacted by this solution?
Client:	No.
You:	Does this impact your strategic plan or goals?
Client:	Yes, reducing costs is one of our key priorities this year.
You:	What has stopped you from moving forward in the past?
Client:	This has not been a priority and never investigated.
You:	Are you faced with deadlines?
Client:	No specific deadlines for this.
You:	Who will be involved with implementing a solution?
Client:	I can't spare anyone to work fulltime on this.

You:	What investment are you planning to make in the solution?
Client:	We were thinking $50,000.
You:	I believe we can deliver a solution that will meet all your needs and expectations.
	Correct me if I am mistaken. The key issues you have are lost inventory, etc. Based on the data you have collected, if you do nothing, this issue will cost you $1 million per year. You would like to: keep lost inventory below 2% etc… and based on your analysis this would save your company $2 million per year. Is this correct?
Client:	Yes, what you have stated is exactly what we are looking for.
You:	What are your thoughts about a solution that looks something like this? The combination of new software, processes improvements and training will deliver …. We can provide all the staffing resources for you. The solution can be delivered in 6 months which will meet your strategic plan goals and start delivering dramatic cost reductions. The investment made in this solution will be $200,000 returning $2,000,000 in cost reductions each year. The payback period is less than 2 months, with an ROI of… (listing other value benefits.).
Client:	Client considers the need vs. solution.
Client:	This is a much bigger problem than we realized. Even though the solution is more costly than we thought, the value returned is well worth the investment. Let's move forward with this solution.

Wow! Doesn't a value based technique change the dynamics of the conversation and eliminate all objections and resistance? Even though this was a shortened and simplified example, you can see the power of this technique. Throughout the process your client defines the solution and the value it will deliver. It's hard for him or her to object to the data he or she provides. You can also see how you can address success barriers in your solution so that they don't become objections.

Try out this technique with your next client. You will be amazed at how much more business you get-- quicker and at a higher revenue when you're not dealing with client objections and resistance.

Turn Weaknesses Into Strengths

There will always be a few valid client objections that you cannot ignore and must overcome. Your client has a need that your product or service can't meet. Your competitor has a clear advantage that you have not overcome. These objections will occur over the course of your career and you have no control to stop them. However, what I can do right now is show you how to achieve the best possible outcome.

I call this "turning weaknesses into strengths". To win more business by turning your weaknesses into strengths, you need to start building a list of talking points that cover any and all weakness objections that you may confront. These are perceived weaknesses about you, your product and service, or your company which may come up as a client objection. Above in "Understanding Signals" we listed 27 objection items. Some of these might be perceived weaknesses working against you. When sitting in front of a client, you need to be fully prepared to discuss these objections. When you are prepared, you can turn their objection into a positive outcome.

Here is how it works.

1. Create a List of Your Weaknesses
Put together a list of what could be perceived by your clients as a weakness about you, your product, service or company. Start with the 27 items we described earlier and add others that apply. Think back to all the objections you have encountered over the past year. Put those on the list. Be honest with yourself. Include everything. For example, as a small startup company you might have objections that you are too small and not financially stable.

2. Create a List Of Your Strengths

Compile a list of your strengths. A good place to start is to research your competitors and determine their weaknesses. Look at criteria such as their products, services, financials and organizational structure. Compare how you are positioned against your competitors. From this list of competitor weaknesses, start building a list of your strengths. Add in other strengths that you have which are not related to your competitors. For example, you might be the first company to deploy a new technology that dramatically reduces storage costs.

3. Create a Talking Points Lists

Now that you have a consolidated list of your weaknesses and strengths, you are ready to create a talking points list. First, list all weaknesses in the left hand column. Then prioritize them with the biggest weakness first, second largest second, etc. In the right hand column, next to each weakness, describe how this weakness is really a strength for your organization. For example, here is a simplified sample list:

Weakness	Strength
1. Your company is too small	As a small firm we are able to focus more on personal service. Larger companies are not able to provide this.
2. Your company is financially new	As a new company to this market we are able to provide you with more aggressive competitive pricing.

This talking points list should become a living, breathing document that you update regularly. It should be available to everyone in your organization and reviewed prior to all client meetings. By turning your weaknesses into strengths, you can now turn client objections and resistance into a position of strength. End result--more clients will sign larger contracts in a shorter sales cycle.

Handling the "Price" Objection

If most of the objections you are getting focus on the cost of your product/service, then most likely you're not digging deep enough for their challenges, examples and expectations. Therefore, you're not able to show the client the value of your solution. What you want to do is help the client rationalize and justify the needed investment in your solution. If you have done your best with the information above and still get the "price" objection, follow it with this response:

Client: I can get this cheaper at another company.

You: I completely understand that you are very concerned with the cost of this solution and want to get the most value for your money. (From this statement they will feel you have their best interest at heart and will listen fully to your next statements.)

You: I think you will agree that the lowest price isn't always the best value. Most of us look for three things when making a large investment: great quality, excellent service and the lowest price. I haven't run into a company yet that can provide great quality and excellent service at the lowest price. I'm curious, which one of the three are you most willing to give up: quality, service or low price?

You will find that most of your clients will not give up great quality. Many will not give up excellent service; therefore, that only leaves price. When they can finally come to the conclusion that your product/service offers them value instead of lowest price, they will realize the decision has already been made for them.

Bonus Tips and Techniques

1. Objections Start Early
Very few clients will have objections to your questions. Most objections target your proposed solution that, in their mind, doesn't meet a need. If you are getting objections early in the sales cycle

then it probably means you are leading the discussions with features, capabilities and solutions. Don't talk about any solutions until you have asked all your questions in an attempt to uncover the client's challenges, examples, expectations and success barriers.

2. Leave Your Ego at Home

When a client confronts you with an objection, resists your proposal or plainly say "no", it's not directed to you personally. For some reason, the client is not sold on the value you can deliver. Don't get defensive. And under no circumstances, do not argue with the client. Be pleasant at all times and tactful with your responses during these situations.

3. Stating the Obvious

Sometimes you will run into situations where you are getting verbal or non-verbal objection signals and you don't know how to respond. When this happens, many top performers follow a simple three step plan. Their goal is to state the obvious issue and ask the client what they think we should do next.

1. Opening Statement: "I am confused." Or "I think we may have a problem" or "I am concerned about something here."
2. State the concern.
3. Ask the client what they think we should do next.

Let's take a look at an example:

1. Jim, I am concerned about something here.
2. You said this solution will save your company $5 million per year, but you are not willing to invest $500,000 in the solution.
3. What do you think we should do?

Give this a try the next time you're confronted with this situation. Your client just might resolve their own objection.

My Top Book Recommendations

If you would like to research this topic in more detail, I highly recommend the following books.

- Selling 101: What Every Successful Sales Professional Needs to Know, by Zig Ziglar, ISBN-13: 978-0785264811

- How to Win Friends & Influence People, by Dale Carnegie, ISBN-13: 978-0671027032

- How to Close Every Sale, by Joe Girard, ISBN-13: 978-0446389297

What will you learn next?

In the next chapter we focus on how you can overcome your fear of speaking in public and develop a presentation that will inspire and motivate your audience into action.

4. Persuade and Motivate Your Audience

Influencing the thinking and behavior of your client is your primary goal when you present ideas and recommendations. To successfully influence and persuade your audience, you will need to stand up and present your ideas to a room of people. Research surveys show that most professionals fear this type of public speaking more than death. Worry no longer. I will show you how to overcome your fears and give you the tools to persuade and motivate your audience into action.

In this chapter you will learn:

- □ 4 areas where you must exceed expectations to make a great impression;
- □ 3 critical elements of persuasion;
- □ 5 organization and planning steps that get maximum results;
- □ 4 bonus speaking tips from top performers.

Overcoming Your Fear of Public Speaking

Research surveys indicate that most professionals fear public speaking more than death. I don't believe most professionals would rather die instead of speaking to a group, but this does demonstrate why so many professionals have trouble speaking in front of clients. Based on my personal experience of working with thousands of sales, service and consulting professionals, I believe only 15% of them actually enjoy speaking to groups. The other 85% are not comfortable communicating in person, and when they must, they prefer reading canned questions or presentations that sour the client's experience.

A frustrated Executive VP of Sales for a large software company called me last quarter. His entire sales organization (10,000 product sales professionals) completed a new sales training program six months earlier. Instead of expected increases, his sales numbers were declining. I agreed to help this executive uncover potential reasons for this unanticipated dip.

After meeting with the management team, training department and random sales teams we concluded that the sales training did not address a core communication skill- speaking in front of client groups. The company had assumed for years that sales professionals were fantastic speakers, after all, they are sales people. To make this worse, the training provided everyone with canned presentations, speaking points and questions. They were to use these as a framework when talking with clients. This resulted in thousands of sales professionals reading line by line from the canned material. This was definitely not a great method of inspiring or persuading their clients. In the entire history of the organization, sales professionals were never taught how to organize and deliver a powerful and inspiring message. In the end, they wasted millions of dollars to create a message that delivered no value to the organization. The key missing component was to teach the sales force how to overcome the fear of speaking to large and small client groups.

Does this sound familiar in your organization?

When you embrace the challenge of speaking in front of large groups, you will have a major advantage over your peers and competitors, positioning yourself with top performers in your industry. To start, all you need is a small push.

Get Started Today

You might be more comfortable communicating with clients via email or by phone rather than in person. Presenting to a small group in person might give you a nervous stomach that feels like jagged broken glass tearing you up. This is normal. To become a top performer, you need to overcome your fear and understand the importance of speaking skills. The ability to verbally communicate is one of the most vital communication skills. Top performers need to communicate clearly, confidently, and inspire and persuade large and small groups. They learned early what most people haven't- speaking is fun and easy once you learn the secrets to organization and delivery.

Let's explore these secrets now.

Impression Counts More Than You Think

Impressions are critical in business today. This is especially true when speaking to clients one-on-one or to large groups. Your client must like and respect you before he or she will accept your ideas. Your content and message is important, but the client's opinion of you is of equal importance for you to be successful.

Clients must view you as one of their own- someone whose interests are the same as theirs. Your success will be determined by how well you exceed their expectations in the following areas:

1. Conviction
You present your ideas or recommendations with sincerity and truly believe what you are presenting will deliver value to the client.

Clients do not trust outsiders, especially consultants and sales professionals. You must make it perfectly clear that your ideas are in the client's best interest.

2. Reputation

Accomplishments and past performance form the basis for your reputation. Clients should be familiar with your reputation before hearing your ideas or recommendations. Send them information on your qualifications prior to your meeting or review during your introduction. Focus on the qualifications that are relevant to the client's industry and business and provide them with some concrete examples of how you have achieved success in this particular sector.

3. Expertise

You must be qualified to discuss the clients industry, business and challenges. You must have knowledge of the subject, challenges, solutions and able to provide plenty of evidence supporting your ideas and recommendations. Real life examples provide the best supporting evidence.

4. Appearance

If you appear shy and nervous, your clients will be less likely to accept your ideas or recommendations. Speak firmly, confidently and look directly into the eyes of everybody in the room.

Persuading Your Clients

Influencing the thinking or behavior of the client is your primary goal when you present your ideas. There are three ways to accomplish this. When you organize your material for a meeting or presentation, incorporate the following three elements of persuasion.

1. Inspire Your Client

Your objective is to excite the client about your ideas and beliefs. Connect with his or her feelings, fears and goals. Explain how and why the current situation is changing and the benefits they will achieve in the end.

2. Convince Your Client

Changing a client's mind is difficult. Your client might already think he or she has the answer or a rational view of the subject. To convince your client, you must provide evidence from outside resources that support your position. Emotions also play a role. You must arouse emotions such as happiness, sadness fear, anger or guilt. And finally, clients want to know, "What's in it for me?"

3. Get Your Client to Take Action

You want your client to take some kind of action at the end of your talk. This could be scheduling the next meeting, reviewing a proposal, signing a letter of intent or signing a contract. To make this happen, you need to ask for the action or next steps. Directly ask the client how they would like to proceed or propose the next steps that you need to take.

Inspire Your Clients

Inspiring clients requires you to talk to either an existing or unrecognized desire, need or concern. When you tap into these, you will be able to inspire your client.

Inspiration is more emotional than logical. Your presentation must:
- connect with the clients feelings;
- explain how and why the situation is changing;
- motivate and challenge the client to adopt change and elaborate on the advantages of change.

For example, let's say you have recommended a major reorganization. You want your presentation to inspire employees to embrace the reorganization to help the company become more successful.

Employees will be concerned about their jobs. They will ask questions such as: Will I have a job? Will it drastically change? Will I be demoted? Are my skills still important? Will there be opportunities for promotion? Before you can inspire the employees to embrace the reorganization you must address these concerns first. You want to assure them their jobs are secure, they are valued, and the company recognizes their contributions. Once the employees realize you understand their concerns, they will be more receptive to the reorganization.

Your next step will be to explain the changes and why they are happening. Finally, you need to address what the employees can do to help support these changes and elaborate on the benefits they will see from the reorganization. Appeal to their pride and professionalism toward their work and the company. Then reenergize their enthusiasm and commitment to the company.

Organize for Results

Your clients will be more responsive to your ideas and recommendations if you take the time to organize your thoughts in a logical manner. Organized presentations are easy to understand and remember, are credible and are enjoyable.

The first step in preparing a powerful presentation is to assemble your ideas into a logical sequence that will help you achieve your goals. The following outline will help you plan your key points and organize them in the most effective sequence.

1. Duration
Determine how much time you have to talk. Make sure you consider time allocated to introductions before you present and questions and answers afterwards. This can eat into your overall time "on stage". Once you find out exactly how much time you have to speak, you can then plan accordingly.

2. Client Profile
Who is your audience? Are you talking to a room of business executives, engineers or doctors? Or, is the client a mix between managers and end users? Your presentation purpose, main points and conclusion must focus on the needs of the client's profile.

3. Purpose

A clearly defined, specific purpose statement will make your presentation more focused and beneficial for your client. The purpose is a single sentence that summarizes your presentation goal. This statement will describe your key message and action points.

Your purpose statement must be written from the client's point of view. What do you want the client to gain or take action on after hearing your presentation? Keep your wording clear and concise. The purpose should also be realistic. After your presentation, the client should be able to easily recall the purpose and main points supporting the purpose.

Purpose Examples:
- After hearing my presentation, the management team will approve the proposal to build a new distribution center.
- After hearing my presentation, you will be able to identify four necessary steps to increase customer retention.

4. Topic Title

Attract clients to your presentation with an attention grabbing title. How many times have you used a title like, "Reducing Inventory" or "New Inventory Software"? Most clients would pass on attending a presentation with such a lame title. What would be the value for them to attend such an event? If you are lucky, they might send an underling to the presentation to learn more.

To make an impact on your clients and excite them about attending your presentation, you need to treat your topic title like a newspaper headline. Headlines sell newspapers and they will do the same for you. You need a compelling topic title headline that focuses on the client's challenges.

Your topic title should:
- be less than 15 words long;
- avoid technical jargon;

- address your client's challenges or interests;
- be written from the clients point of view;
- describe a tangible benefit or value they will gain;
- be time specific if possible.

Topic Title Examples:
- "Reduce Inventory Levels 25% Within 1 Year"
- "Increase Customer Retention in 4 Easy Steps"
- "Improve Customer Satisfaction While Reducing Your Cost of Sales 17%"

Powerful topic titles like these will peak the interest of your clients and more than likely drive up attendance with their eagerness to learn more.

5. Opening

Capture the client's attention immediately by drawing them into your topic and driving home the value they will receive.

Good openings follow one of these formats:
- A startling question or statement
- A challenging question or statement
- A story or illustration relevant to the topic
- An attention grabbing statement that ties into your topic

Avoid weak openings that are common by most professionals:
- A joke
- An apologetic statement
- A general observation
- A long irrelevant story

You now have your client's attention and they are sitting on the edge of their seats. You must follow this strong opening with your supporting facts and ideas.

6. Main Points

The body of your presentation outline contains main points, supporting points and supporting material. The main points contain the key ideas you want your client to retain. Most clients will only remember a maximum of five key points or ideas. First, jot down a list of all the points you want to convey to your client. Second, select three to five of the most important points you want to present to the client. Third, arrange those points in the order that will be most effective in fulfilling your topic purpose.

Example of Main Points:
If you were writing a presentation on the benefits of joining a fitness gym, the three main points you might select are:
- Improve Your Overall Health
- Improve Your Mood
- Meet New Friends

The next step is to elaborate on your main points with supporting points. Supporting points emphasize, clarify or proves the idea you are presenting. Supporting points help the client remember the main point and make the presentation interesting.

Example Supporting Points:
Supporting points for "Improve Your Overall Heath" might be:
- Losing Weight
- Improve Your Cardio System
- Increase Muscle Strength
- Reduce Your Cholesterol

The final step is providing supporting material to backup and support your main and supporting points. Supporting material provides the proof behind your ideas. This material comes in many forms. Select the items that are most appropriate for your client or topic.

These materials include:
- Facts – Verifiable information from personal experience or outside resources.

- Case Studies – Client examples or stories that relate an event relevant to the topic.
- Statistics – Numerical data conveying information in percentage points, averages, etc.
- Testimonials – Quotes from experts or other clients.
- Visualization – Diagrams, pictures, charts or objects supporting your ideas and topic.

The final step in organizing a powerful presentation is to develop a strong conclusion.

7. Conclusion

Finally, persuade and motivate your client to take action. The conclusion should reinforce your ideas/recommendations and leave the client with a clear lasting impression. You should review your main points, summarize your recommendations and value and suggest a course of action for the client. Final remarks may be appropriate and would include a final closing statement, challenge, question, or quotation. Finish upbeat and confident.

Bonus Power Speaking Tips

1. Keep It Short and Sweet

Success ultimately depends on the client's understanding of the words you use. Words are very powerful. They communicate your ideas and are the basis for how the client perceives you and your ideas. Simple, clear and vivid words will add excitement and will help your clients remember your key points. Construct and deliver your presentation following these two simple rules:

Rule One: Keep Your Words Short - Professionals believe they impress clients when they use long, unique words. This is not the case. Top performers understand the most effective and memorable words are short-one or two syllables. Shorter words are more memorable, easier to follow and remember. This is not to say that you should always avoid using longer words.

Rule Two: Keep Your Sentences Short - Shorter sentences are easier to say and easier for the client to understand. They also make a bigger impact. To add variety in your presentation, throw in longer sentences that are easy to follow. To determine if a sentence is too long, look for commas. More than one comma indicates the sentence is too long for your presentation.

2. Speak With Confidence
A lack of confidence causes severe nervousness and will destroy the effectiveness of your presentation. Lack of preparation causes lack of confidence. When you are knowledgeable, interested, have strong feelings and are enthusiastic about your topic you will deliver a confident presentation. An audience receives a confident speaker as convincing and sincere. This gives you credibility with the client. As a result, your client is more willing to accept your ideas and recommendations.

You can use normal nervous energy to your benefit. This can add excitement to your presentation. Let your client feel your enthusiasm and energy. This should, in turn, pump them up as well.

3. Effective Use of Notes
Conveying confidence, enthusiasm, and sincerity to your audience is critical in your delivery. By relying on notes, you might convey the opposite impression to your clients. Maintaining eye contact with your client rather than your notes is the most effective way to deliver your ideas and gain confidence with your client.

Not ready to eliminate notes entirely? The next best method is to use note cards. Write your main points in large letters on a single note card in bullet point format. You can then take a quick glance at each card which will allow you to maintain eye contact with the client.

What Should You Avoid?
- Notepads – They are bulky and distracting.
- Loose 8 ½ X 11 paper – These are noisy and distracting.

- Computer Screen – The client will not be able to see your body language.

4. Avoid Technical Jargon

You can lose your client's attention with one word. If you include technical jargon, buzz words or sports metaphors that are not familiar to your client, they will not grasp your ideas. Speak to your client in a language they are familiar with and understand. Review your client profile to determine whether your words will be appropriate.

My Top Book Recommendations

If you would like to research this topic in more detail, I highly recommend the following books.

- Clear and to the Point: 8 Psychological Principles for Compelling PowerPoint Presentations, by Stephen M. Kosslyn, ISBN-13: 978-0195320695

- Presenting to Win: The Art of Telling Your Story, by Jerry Weissman, ISBN-13: 978-0130464132

- The Exceptional Presenter: A Proven Formula to Open Up and Own the Room, by Timothy J. Koegel, ISBN-13: 978-1929774449

What will you learn next?

In the next chapter we focus on how you can deliver your presentation in a way that will excite your audience. Your recommendations should leave them with a positive lasting impression.

5. Delivering Awesome Speeches and Presentations

You have overcome your fear of talking in front of groups. You have also organized the content of your presentation that is sure to get your point across to the audience. Now what? You need to effectively deliver your message in a way that will excite your audience about your recommendations and leave them with a positive lasting impression. You can accomplish this by following a handful of tips and techniques used by leading speakers and top performers.

In this chapter you will learn:
- [ ] 5 ways to use your body effectively
- [ ] 5 ways to persuade with your voice
- [ ] 6 visualization design techniques that make an impact
- [ ] 7 visualization display techniques that get your point across
- [ ] 7 ways to involve the audience

Talk with Your Body

Your body language communicates confidence, power and excitement. Your body language speaks volumes to those with whom you interact. Your body language helps create a rapport with people and can increase their belief and trust in you.

Imagine attending a promotional kickoff meeting where the speakers goal is to inspire and excite the audience about a new product line. The speaker stands stiffly, does not move or engage in eye contact with the audience. His words indicate he is excited, but his body language proves the opposite. How does this affect you? This negative body language does not encourage you to become motivated to sell that new product.

Your body language will have the same affect on your clients. Excite them about your topic. Inspire them with your ideas and recommendations.

Let's take a look at the five body language expressions and their impact on your client.

1. Moving Around
Movement during your presentation attracts your client's attention and involves them as their eyes follow you from one position to another. It also adds variety for the client.

Your first opportunity to display body language is when you leave your seat and walk to the front of the room. You want to appear eager and confident. Walk at a purposeful quick pace with your head up and shoulders back. When you complete your presentation, walk back the same way.

During your talk, begin speaking in one spot, then move two or three steps as you move on to another topic point. This movement helps provide transition between main points. To emphasize critical points, step toward your client. To dramatize a point, act out your description just before your verbal description. For example, if you are describing a very cold situation, you might act out shivering right before the description.

Below is a list of distracting movements that you should avoid.
- Pacing
- Fidgeting
- Swaying from side to side
- Bouncing up and down

2. Standing in Place
We just discussed moving around during your presentation but there are times when you will be standing in place. During your opening and closing, your stance is important because it indicates your comfort level, confidence and poise. To be most effective, stand with your feet slightly apart and your weight evenly distributed.

Avoid habits that indicate shyness, weakness, nervousness or being uncomfortable.
- Eyes fixed on the floor or ceiling
- Slouching shoulders
- Shifting weight from one foot to the other

3. Eye Contact
Eye contact plays a significant role in how your client perceives you. While speaking, you should pay special attention to how your eyes interact with the client.

Have you ever been in the client's seat, where another speaker was talking and would not look at you directly? The speaker looked at the floor, ceiling or back wall and never directly at you. Did you get the impression he or she was less than honest and lacked confidence? Did he or she inspire or persuade you to back his or her ideas? I don't think so.

When you make eye contact with a client, he or she feels you are honest, credible and sincere. Clients are then more willing to accept and back your ideas. Another benefit from good eye contact is the bonding it creates. As your eyes meet, you get their undivided attention and they will have a hard time ignoring you.

During your presentation, look directly at your clients. Look directly into the eyes of one person until you finish a thought and then move on to another. Make eye contact with clients randomly throughout the entire room. If the room is small you will most likely be able to make direct eye contact with each client in the room. If the room is large and packed, you will not be able to make eye contact with everyone. In this case, make direct eye contact with someone in each section of the room, front, middle, back, right side and left side.

Avoid these bad habits:
- Gazing around the room, no direct eye contact
- Moving your head back and forth like an oscillating fan, distracting the client
- Staring at one person for a long time, making them uncomfortable
- Glancing quickly from one person to the other, making you look untrustworthy

4. Facial Expressions
Your face conveys how your client should react or feel about the information you are presenting. Your facial expressions must be consistent and demonstrate those feelings. If you are talking about achieving record profits, yet you are frowning with your head hung low, your clients will be confused, not excited and happy with the results.

Show happiness and excitement by smiling broadly. Show sadness by frowning slightly and bowing your head. Widening your eyes and raising your eyebrows will display surprise. When you display these feelings, your client will then emulate them.

5. Hand and Arm Gestures

Gestures provide the most expressive body language and help drive home key topic points. The most effective gestures are those made above the elbow and away from your body. They should be definite and vigorous to show your enthusiasm and conviction. The same movement is very distracting, therefore vary your gestures. For larger rooms, these gestures should be even larger to ensure everyone in the back can see them.

Try some of these gestures the next time you are speaking to a client:

- Repeat an up and down motion of your head indicating approval.
- Clench your fist indicating power or anger.
- Hit your clenched fist into an open palm indicating an important point being made.
- Open your palms indicating generosity and caring.
- Fold your arms across your chest indicating strength and determination.
- Clasp your hands in front of your chest indicating unity.
- Move both hands in unison indicating similarities.
- Move your hands in opposite directions indicating differences.

Gestures can mean many things and will vary culture to culture. So, be sensitive to what is acceptable in your client's environment and culture.

Persuading Listeners with Your Voice

What kind of voice do you have? Is it easy to listen to, exciting, deep and rich? Your voice is how you convey information to your clients and gain their acceptance. If your voice is annoying, clients stop paying attention and they will not hear your ideas.

Top performers have four voice characteristics that gain the client's full attention.

- Easily heard - They clearly articulate words and use proper volume.
- Pleasant - They convey friendliness.
- Natural - They project sincerity, reflecting their personality.
- Expressive - They demonstrate various meanings, never emotionless or monotone.

Balancing the levels of extremes between your voice quality, speed, pitch, volume and silence is also critical for successful delivery.

1. Quality

Your voice should be easy to listen to. It should be enjoyable, friendly, and natural. If your voice is harsh or nasal you need to eliminate the tension in your voice.

2. Speed

Speak fast and your client won't be able to keep up. Speak slowly and he or she will lose interest. Keeping your presentation at approximately 125 to 160 words per minute will be fast enough to keep his or her attention and slow enough for him or her to digest your ideas. This is not to say you should speak at a constant rate the entire time. Slow down to emphasize a main point. Speed up through other less important material.

3. Pitch

On the music scale, how high and low your voice sounds is the pitch. Vary your pitch throughout your presentation. Never keep the same monotone voice. This will quickly lull your clients to sleep. On the other end, a constant high pitched voice will make them cover their ears or leave the room.

Adapt your pitch to the topic. For excitement use a higher pitched voice. For sadness use a lower pitched voice.

4. Volume

Controlling the softness and loudness of your voice will keep your clients interested in your topic. Vary your volume level to emphasize key points. Increase the volume for anger or making a final point. Decrease the volume when being secretive or sad. Also remember that your volume depends on the size of the room. Adjust accordingly.

5. Silence

Well placed silences or pauses in your presentation will have a tremendous impact on your words and the points you are making. This is a very powerful speaking tool that presenters do not use enough.

Use silence to:
- Emphasize - Silence before and after a critical statement tells the client this is an important point;
- Punctuate - Silence tells the client you have completed a thought;
- Gain Attention - When clients are losing interest, insert a pause. This pause will attract their attention.

Make a Visual Impact

Clients remember best what they see and hear simultaneously. Do not use visual aids to replace your presentation or create a crutch for lack of preparation. Visual aids should complement and enhance your presentation. Charts, graphs, diagrams and other visually objects will increase clients' retention of your ideas and recommendations.

Visual Aid Benefits

1. Reinforcing Topic Points
Use visual aids to show your client what was said or something very important to remember.

2. Increasing Understanding

Clients learn mostly through their eyes not their ears. Visual aids help clients understand things like dimensions, relationships, statistics and other numerical information.

3. Improving Retention

Clients will remember only 10% of what you say. However, when you include visual aids, clients will remember 66% of what they both hear and see.

4. Improving Attention

A client's mind tends to wander during presentations because he or she thinks much faster than you talk. Visual aids keep their minds focused on you.

5. Communicating Faster

You can communicate faster and better when using visual aids rather than spoken words.

Popular Visualization Tools

Common visualization tools today include an actual product, a computer generated image(s), flip charts and white boards. The best choice for your client will depend on several factors:

- Client profile
- Topic points you want to emphasize
- Type of information you wish to display
- Equipment available

Let's explore these visual aids in more detail. These guidelines will help you select the correct visual aid for your purposes.

1. Product

A product can be an actual product you are recommending. It can also be an object that helps you make a point or helps the client better understand and remember your ideas. You will need to consider the size of the object and the space available in your room.

You may need a table to place the product and a cloth to cover it until you need it.

2. Computer Generated Images
Computer based visualization is becoming standard for most presentations. Using a notebook computer, software and LCD projector, you can produce and display dramatic visuals with a click of the mouse. You can present simple as well as very complex information. Your visual options include presentation slides, pictures, software applications, or video.. You can also walk around the room talking while changing your visuals using a remote control. This allows you more freedom to use gestures and movement while you talk. Here are some points to consider when using computer generated visuals:

- Do you have the equipment or should it be rented?
- Do you have the skills to develop the visuals or should you outsource this?
- Plan enough time to create the visuals in advance.
- Make sure all components work together. Rehearse before your planned presentation date.
- Have a backup plan in case you have technical difficulties before or during your presentation (yes, this does happen).

3. Flip Charts
Flip charts are great for small room briefings, training or brainstorming sessions. Use them to display key topic points or recording client responses. You can prepare pages in advance allowing you the flexibility to add items during your presentation. Writing down information during your presentation helps reinforce points and improve client retention. You can also tear off pages and hang them on the walls for easy viewing. An added benefit with flip charts is you can review the actual recording of key topic points, questions, and issues at a later time.

4. White Boards

White boards are very common in meeting rooms. They work well when you need to display your key topic points or make small lists. However, there are a few drawbacks. If the white board is not cleaned well, it is difficult to read. Markers dry out quickly so you need to test them to make sure there is sufficient ink to produce readable script. Finally, there is no way to save the information on the white board. If you need to document this information, you need to transcribe it onto your notebook computer or paper.

Visualization Design Tips

Effective visual aids are pleasing to view, easy to understand and easy to read. Consider these top performer tips when developing your visual aids.

1. Visible

Make sure everyone in the room can easily see your visual aid. Use the largest letters possible. Use blank space to make the words more visible. Make sure letter, diagram or picture coloring is not similar to the background color. You want your items to stand out. For example, yellow letters on a black background really add punch to the visual.

2. One Topic Point

Limit each visual to one main topic point or idea. Clients are distracted when viewing more than one.

3. 6X6 Method

Have no more than 6 words and 6 lines per visual. This allows you to keep the letters large, easy and quick to read. Your client will then be able to focus on you as the speaker.

4. Add Variety

Variety in your visuals will maintain the client's interest. If you use a computer slide show, don't show just text or just diagrams on the slides. Create variety and mix it up a bit. For example, follow a text slide with a diagram or chart.

5. Eye Candy

Use consistent style formats for fonts, color, and artwork. This provides consistency in the visual which is more pleasing and enjoyable to the client's eye.

6. Simple

Your clients should be able to identify the point quickly. Avoid using fancy graphics or multiple diagrams clustered together.

Visualization Display Tips

There are many things that can go wrong when you display your visuals. Each of these tips will lessen the impact of your message and lower your credibility. Let's examine a few top performer tips that will help you deliver a memorable visual presentation.

1. Display before Talking

Display your visual aid before you start talking about it. The moment you display your visual aid the client will focus on absorbing the content and will not be listening to you.. Display your visual aid, pause while the client absorbs the content, and then begin talking.

2. Keep Client Eye Contact

Maintain eye contact with your client (don't turn your back on them) while displaying your visual aid. Don't face the visual aid and read from it. This shows your client that you are not prepared and you will lose credibility with them.

3. Timely Removal

Display your visual aid long enough to discuss the topic point it supports. When complete, remove it from view. When you use flip charts, make sure you have a blank page between visuals. When you finish one page, flip to the next (blank) page. If you are using a notebook computer and PowerPoint slides, have a blank slide between visuals or hit the "B" key to turn the screen black. To redisplay the slide hit the "B" key again.

4. Don't Block the View
Every client in the room must be able to view your visual aid. Stand to the side or your visual aid. If you need to point something out, use a pointer or your hand. If you are displaying a product that you can pick up, hold it to the left or right of your body at shoulder height.

5. Don't Talk and Write
When writing on a white board or flip chart, don't talk while you are writing. When you finish writing, turn back to the client and begin speaking.

6. Be Ready
Prior to your presentation, put all the visual aids in their appropriate spot. Check their positioning to make sure everyone will have a clear view. Triple check all electronic equipment to make sure it is functioning properly. Don't forget backup batteries.

7. Practice
Confidence and composure will be your key to effective presentations. The more you practice, the more familiar you are with your voice and material, the more comfortable you'll be in front of the client.

If you have access to a tape or digital recorder, use it to record your practice sessions. Review the results and make changes that will improve your effectiveness. Your voice should be natural and consistent with the meaning of the material. Listen for your voice volume, speed, pitch, quality and appropriate pauses for affect. Make notes on where and how these can be improved.

Practice in front of a mirror to improve your body language. Does your body language show confidence, power and excitement? Does it enhance your credibility and emphasize your main points and recommendations. Watch your head, arm and hand movements. Make sure you move around.

Persuading Your Client with Involvement

More than 70% of the presentations I've witnessed are missing a key component for achieving client buy-in. This component is client involvement. Involving your client is one of the most powerful ways to persuade him or her and ultimately get him or her to say "yes" to your request or "I agree" with your point of view.

Why are presenters not involving the client? Here are a few examples. Have you used these excuses at one time or another?
- I am not comfortable interacting with the client.
- I did not have enough time to prepare.
- I don't know the best way to involve the client.
- I'm nervous enough already, why add unpredictable components?

If you want to dramatically increase your success by persuading your clients, try inserting a few of these "Involvement" strategies into your next presentation.

1. Ask a thought provoking question
Ask the client an open ended question that makes him or her use his or her imagination or reflect on a current situation. There is no right or wrong answer for this type of question. For example, "What could you accomplish if you had an additional 2 hours of uninterrupted time a day?"

2. Raise your hand if...
This involvement technique will involve your client and also provide visual support for the client response. You could ask, "Raise

your hand if you have ever worked for an unreasonable manager?" "As you can see from the response, nine out of ten of you have had this unfortunate experience."

3. Multiple choice question

Ask a question about your topic and provide the client with a list of possible answers. This technique makes it easier to answer and still makes the client put some thought into his or her response. For example, "How many technology projects are considered successful? A) 23%, B) 37%, C) 62% or D) 99%." Your client will retain this information longer by putting some thought into his or her answer and will be more comfortable answering since they have a one in four chance of being correct.

4. Fill in the answer

Studies show that you are more likely to remember important facts if you write them down. A great way to ensure your client records key information is to provide presentation handouts with fill the blank answers. For example, you might have a slide that reads "Implementing this unique sales approach can improve sales revenue by _____%, equivalent to a $_____ increase in sales this year". This is a great technique that energizes your client while helping him or her retain the critical facts you are presenting.

5. Ask a simple question

Nobody wants to look foolish in front of a crowd. By asking easy questions that are focused on your client's experience, you will see audience participation increase. When everyone is involved in the discussion, people will be more enthusiastic and also have the opportunity to learn from their peers. You might ask a question like, "What is your number one priority this year?" or "What leadership skill do you think is most important?"

6. Hand out a questionnaire

Writing answers down is much more powerful than trying to remember the answer. Provide your client with a short questionnaire that list three to five open ended questions that are relevant to your discussion. This provides him or her with valuable personal insight he or she can take back to the office and work with the following day. For example, if you were delivering a presentation on starting a small business, you might ask questions like: 1) What is your product? 2) Who is your competition? 3) Who will be your target customers?

7. End with an action plan

Every presentation should end with a client action plan, that is, some take-away where the client can use the information you presented. One of the best tools is the "Action Plan". At the end of your presentation, ask the client to take out a pen and paper. At the top of a fresh page, write the words "Action Plan". Under this, list the numbers 1, 2 and 3 so the client can fill in the actions he or she will take right after your presentation. For example, if you present a workshop on technology cost reduction, ask the client to write down the top three actions he or she will take tomorrow to reduce technology costs.

You don't need to include all seven involvement techniques in your presentation. That might overwhelm the client. For shorter presentations you might include two or three of these techniques. Try it. You will see a dramatic increase in positive responses to your topic.

My Top Book Recommendations

If you would like to research this topic in more detail, I highly recommend the following books.

- Public Speaking (8th Edition), by Michael Osborn, Suzanne Osborn, Randall Osborn, ISBN-13: 978-0205584567

- Public Speaking: An Audience-Centered Approach (6th Edition), by Steven A. Beebe, Susan J. Beebe, ISBN-13: 978-0205449835

- There's No Such Thing as Public Speaking: Make Any Presentation or Speech as Persuasive as a One-on-One Conversation, by Jeanette and Roy Henderson, ISBN-13: 978-0735204157

What will you learn next?

In the next chapter we focus on how you can create a culture that holds productive meaningful meetings by focusing on how you organize and prepare for your meetings.

6. The Master Meeting Planner

How many meetings do you hold each day - two, five, maybe eight or more? Are these meetings productive? Holding unproductive meetings creates unhappy clients, lower productivity, reduced performance, and increases your cost of doing business. As a top performer you want to hold meetings that produce tangible results that will impact your business by increasing revenue or reducing costs. To create a culture that delivers meaningful, productive meetings, you will need to start focusing on how you organize and prepare. You need to become a Master Meeting Planner.

In this chapter you will learn:
- 3 reasons why you should call a meeting
- 9 steps for planning an effective meeting
- 13 key elements in the best agendas
- 6 key questions to ask when planning for the best meeting location

Organization Is Key

Joan, a good friend, client and management consultant, called me to discuss an urgent matter. She was working sixty hours a week handling multiple projects that were not going well. She spent the majority of her time, forty hours per week, in meetings that dragged on without any results. Nobody was able to make a decision. Sound familiar? Joan decided it was time to take the lead in order to turn projects around. That was a great first step, but what should she do next?

After reviewing her meeting experiences, Joan clearly recognized that the dynamic, fast paced, ever changing nature of these projects was the challenge. Her solution was to carefully plan and organize in order to obtain highly effective and productive meeting results. After just five days, her new found preparation and organization techniques were so successful, her clients gave her the nickname "Master Meeting Planner".

Let's explore the planning, organization and preparation steps that will help you become the "Master of Meetings".

Understanding The Purpose of "A Meeting"

What is a meeting and why have one? Simply, a meeting is a group of people coming together for the purpose of transacting business.

Meetings are one key element of your business day. They can dramatically move your business forward or hold it back. Unfortunately, it feels like you spend most of your day in meetings that seem, and often are, a complete waste of time. Based on twenty years of personal experience and talking with business owners, consultants, sales professionals and clients around the world, I can tell you that being part of a highly effective meeting is rare. Those who run effective meetings not only know when to meet, they also know "how" to meet. Meeting gurus can make a meeting effective, efficient and downright fun.

Why Are You Holding a Meeting?

There are several basic reasons for holding a meeting. Each one has a unique purpose.

1. Distributing Information

We hold information distribution meetings in order to communicate information, report project updates, pitch products or give and receive feedback. This meeting type is designed to keep the meeting participants updated with the most recent information available.

2. Solving a Problem

You or your client has a defined problem or challenge. You call a meeting to verify the problem definition, investigate solution alternatives and solve the problem. Participants in a problem solving meeting must have a vested interest in the problem and the expertise to solve it.

3. Making a Decision

We hold decision making meetings to select a solution or make a critical decision. Success is dependent on having the "right" decision makers in the room and agreement on the decision making process. A decision making process can be a decision by group consensus, by majority vote or by selected individuals based on input from others.

The need to make a decision is often the driving force to call a meeting. For example, we often hold departmental meetings to provide updated status information and to solve specific problems or challenges

When Should You Have A Meeting?

It's best to call a meeting when you:

- have a problem and need input from different groups with varying perspectives or agendas;
- need clarification on a problem;

- require information or advice from one or more qualified experts;
- want a group of people to participate in making a decision or solving a problem;
- wish to share information or a concern with a group.

When Should You "Not" Have a Meeting?

It's best not to call a meeting when you:

- have a personnel issue that is better handled one-on-one;
- don't have time to prepare properly (see next section);
- are better off communicating in another manner such as a memo, e-mail, or telephone call;
- have already made a decision;
- have a problem or subject that is a low priority and not worth everyone's time;
- have an emotionally upset group that needs time to cool off before addressing the problem or making a decision.

Powerful Meetings Start with Preparation

Powerful and effective meetings are always well thought out in advance. If you don't have time to prepare for a meeting, you should postpone it until you are prepared. Have you ever been involved in a meeting where you didn't know what was being accomplished or, you didn't have the right meeting participants involved? Perhaps the meeting was a free- for- all with no set agenda or structure? Did you think that meeting was effective or successful? Did you accomplish anything? I doubt it. Top performers who run powerful and effective meetings will tell you their success is based primarily on their meeting preparation.

Your preparation begins by 1) planning your meeting, 2) creating a detailed agenda, 3) determining the best location and 4) doing your homework. Let's examine these four preparation steps in more detail.

Planning an Effective Meeting

Organization is the tool of choice for planning an effective and powerful meeting. Here are the steps that will produce a fantastic meeting which will exceed your client's expectations and produce your expected results.

1. What Is The Meeting Purpose?

Successful meeting preparation starts with a clearly defined meeting purpose. Define why you are bringing everyone together. The clearer your purpose, the more effective the meeting will be. As we described in the previous section, are you meeting to make a decision, solve a problem or distribute information? It is imperative for you to define specifically the purpose.

For example:
- Select our new raw materials provider.
- Identify three alternatives for reducing our cost of sales.
- Approve next year's budget revisions.
- Introduce next year's new product strategy.

2. What Is The Expected Outcome?

Clearly define the exact outcome you desire from your meeting. This is usually an extension of your purpose. Ask yourself, "What do I want my meeting participants to say, do or decide?"

For example:
- Select the raw materials vendor that will provide the greatest Return on Investment (ROI)
- Determine our three best cost of sales reduction alternatives.
- Obtain the CEO's final approval on next year's budget revisions.
- Energize our sales force with the new product strategy.

3. Meeting Name

Based on your meeting purpose, outcome and objective, give your meeting an enticing and meaningful name. You can use this name or title as the headline for the meeting. Make it descriptive enough for the participants to identify it with a quick glance.

For example:
- Raw Materials Vendor Selection Meeting
- Cost of Sales Reduction Review Meeting
- Budget Revision Approval Meeting
- New Product Strategy – Energizing Your Sales Team

4. Who Should Attend?

Your meeting purpose, outcome and objective will determine whom you select (delegates) to attend your meeting. Include only enough people to allow you to achieve your objectives. Delegates must be able to add value to your meeting. They should be the decision makers or experts to solve a specific problem, or the group you want to inform. Let's examine a few areas before creating your final attendee list.

Here is a quick checklist to help you determine who should attend your meeting:
- Key decision makers
- Delegates who can give relevant and valuable input
- Delegates who have a stake in the outcome
- Delegates who require the information to do their jobs
- Delegates who will actually implement the decisions

If you are experiencing trouble getting the right people to attend, try these tips:
- Emphasize the benefit and value they will receive by attending.
- Give them an active role in the meeting (described later).
- Invite them personally.
- Set up the meeting date and time that best fits their schedule.

5. What Is The Right Size For Your Meeting?

Your goal is to get the right participants to your meeting. To be effective, they must be able to add value to the discussion, as we discussed above. The number of participants involved is a factor for achieving your meeting outcome. What is the right number of participants? The answer is, from one to infinity, depending on the type of meeting. Okay, that doesn't help much. Let's narrow your meeting size down by type of meeting.

- Distributing Information – If you call a meeting to discuss the status of a project, quarterly results or any meeting to rally your teams, invite everyone. The more participants the better. Don't be shy.

- Problem Solving – If the meeting purpose is to discuss a new challenge and determine alternative solutions, invite no more than 15 participants. These individuals must have relevant expertise in the necessary field or be directly affected by the challenges. Each participant must bring value to the table. Don't expect a solution consensus from this group. Your goal is to present alternatives and possibly, your top three alternative solutions.

- Decision Making – If the meeting purpose is to make a final decision, then invite no more than five participants. These delegates should be the decision makers or key experts who can answer any final questions before making a decision. If you have more than five participants,, it will only add confusion and delay in making a decision.

6. When Should You Hold Your Meeting?

Meetings can be held anytime, day or night, seven days a week. Some times are more optimal than others. Have you ever held a meeting at 2pm on a Saturday? If so, did you get the full attention from your meeting participants? Or, were they day dreaming about golfing, fishing or spending time with their kids?

To schedule your meeting, remember that there are good times and better times.

Rule #1 - Make sure you hold a meeting at a convenient time for the participants. Make sure the meeting does not overlap with other important meetings.

Rule #2 - Try to avoid meeting on weekends. I don't know about you, but I have never attended a weekend meeting that met its purpose and objectives. The only exception would be a company "rah- rah" session that is combined with outside activities and the main purpose is to build morale and have a good time.

Rule #3 - Hold your meeting at the most productive time of day. Many studies indicate that people are at their peak during the workday. Late mornings rise to the top of the list. An optimum time to schedule a meeting is between the hours of 9am and Noon. Late afternoon is another good time. Meetings between 2pm and 5pm are also very productive. My third choice would be an early morning meeting starting around 7am. Early morning meetings can be tricky and will depend on the personal habits of the meeting participants. If your participants are early risers, this might be a very good time to meet.

Rule #4 - From personal experience, Monday mornings and Friday afternoons do not provide the most effective results. If possible, don't hold a decision making or problem solving meeting during these times. Your meeting participants will either be recovering from their weekend or daydreaming about their exciting weekend plans.

Rule #5 - Do not hold critical decision making or problem solving meetings during breakfast, lunch or dinner. These are good times to hold a general information or client relationship (get to know you) meeting. There is just too much activity for anyone to make a sound decision or think through a new business challenge.

7. How Long Should Your Meeting Be?

Business meetings usually last between thirty minutes to three hours. Your goal is to achieve all your objectives in the shortest time possible. Effective and powerful meetings use time efficiently. As a general rule, it will take at least thirty minutes to cover one topic. For the best results, plan your meeting to address no more than four related topics. More than four will overwhelm your meeting participants, limiting your chances for a successful meeting.

8. Where Should You Hold Your Meeting?

Offsite? Onsite? In someone's office or conference room? These are questions to ask yourself. The easiest answer is the location. Your meeting room must be big enough to hold all the participants comfortably. Can you fit ten participants comfortably in the CEO's office? Not likely. Strategic or critical problem solving meetings are most effective when you hold them offsite in a large meeting room. This lessens the interruptions so everyone can focus on the objectives. For decision making meetings and information distribution, a conference room at the client's site is sufficient. Only conduct a meeting in a client's office when the meeting is one- on -one.

9. What Are The Roles Of The Meeting Participants?

As you plan your meeting, make sure you have identified meeting participants to fill the meeting roles. Each meeting participant should fit into one of the following roles. A meeting participant may also fill several roles within the meeting. If a meeting participant does not fit into one of these roles, you must determine if his or her presence is really necessary.

Powerful and effective meeting roles include:
- Host – This participant initiates the meeting He or she ensures that the appropriate attendees are invited and

the meeting agenda is delivered to everyone prior to the meeting.

- Meeting Leader – This participant clarifies the purpose, objectives and expected outcome for the meeting. He or she takes the responsibility for follow-up activities.
- Facilitator – This participant guides the meeting participants through the agenda. He or she ensures all points are covered and that the meeting stays focused. He or she may ask that participants table new issues for another meeting.
- Timekeeper – This participant keeps the meeting on schedule. As time runs out for an agenda item, he or she will inform the group to conclude that agenda item.
- Scribe – This participant documents the key ideas, points and decisions made during the meeting. He or she will also be responsible for drafting the final meeting minutes.
- Specialist – This participant contributes expert knowledge on specific agenda items. The specialist may or may not be present for the entire meeting. He or she may cover one or many items depending on the agenda.
- Contributor – This participant is the primary contributor to the meeting. He or she might be the decision maker or active in the problem-solving discussions.

Planning the Best Agenda

You should create an agenda for all your meetings. The agenda is your outline or roadmap for achieving your meeting purpose, outcome and objectives. Distribute the meeting agenda to all participants prior to the meeting, at least two days prior to the scheduled date. Ideally, it is best to send the agenda out a week ahead of time. This allows your participants an opportunity to better prepare their materials and achieve your expected outcome.

Your meeting agenda should include the following:

- Meeting Name - Official meeting name or title setup by the meeting host. Your meeting name should be descriptive and enticing.

- Meeting Purpose - One of two sentences defining the purpose and objectives of the meeting.

- Expected Outcome - Define the desired outcome or decisions that should occur by the end of this meeting.

- Meeting Date - The date(s) of your meeting.

- Meeting Time - The meeting start and end time.

- Meeting Place - The location of the meeting. This includes the address, building, and meeting room number.

- Hosted By - The name of the meeting owner and host. Include company name and job title.

- Host Contact Information - The phone number and email address of the meeting host. This is helpful if meeting participants need to contact the host prior to the meeting.

- Meeting Participant Roles - For each meeting role assign a participant. Include his or her name, title and company. Assign meeting participants to meeting leader, facilitator, timekeeper, scribe, specialists and contributors.

- Copy To - This is a list of those who will not be attending this meeting but should be copied on the agenda and minutes.

- Agenda Topic List – The agenda items to be covered, including the agenda item owner and time allocated. Always include time on the agenda for introductions, meeting kickoff, review of previous action items, meeting recap and next steps. Studies indicate that productive meetings include a five to ten minute break every fifty minutes. Don't forget breaks in the meeting for everyone to relax and regroup. When organizing your topics, reduce complex topics into manageable parts. Begin the meeting with a simple topic and then gradually work your way to more complex topics. Sequence your agenda items so that they build upon each other.

- General Background – Provide a brief summary on the background of previous meetings concerning this topic.

- Previous Action Item Updates – List all issues and action items from the previous meeting that you will review at the beginning of the meeting.

At this point, most of my clients say, "Wow! That is an incredible amount of information for a meeting agenda." Yes, this is true, compared to the weak agendas we often see at poorly planned meetings. To lead an effective power meeting, you need to be organized and prepared. That is why top performers use an agenda format like the one we just described.

Planning For the Right Setting

Your meeting objectives, number and type of meeting participants will determine your setting. Poor settings can ruin critical meetings. You must treat your meeting setting as important as the meeting material. If one is lacking, the entire meeting can fail.

When planning the location and setting for your meeting, ask yourself the following:

1. Which Location Is Best?
You may want to hold the meeting at your location if you have "value add" material that is only accessible at your location. For a

large group you might consider an offsite location such as a hotel or resort meeting room. This provides you with a neutral location with minimal interruptions and also serves as a base if you plan additional activities after the meeting. The most common meeting place is the client's location. This allows the client to meet in his or her comfort zone (home court) and gives him or her a perception of greater control.

2. What Size Room Do I Need?

Don't skimp on seating or display area. Have you ever attended a meeting where you felt as though you were sitting on each other's lap? Instead of paying attention to the speaker or participating, you can only think about how you can escape. Cramped quarters will detract from your meeting effectiveness. When selecting a room, take the number of invited participants and multiply by 20%. This will give you enough space for everyone to spread out and participate comfortably.

3. How Should The Room Be Arranged?

If you have products to display, make sure there is an open spot in the room that everyone can easily see. If you want to encourage open communication, place the tables in a large horseshoe so everyone can see each other. If you will be breaking out into smaller workgroups, use round tables.

4. What Technical Equipment Is Needed?

Will you need a laptop computer, LCD projector, video phone, conference phone, microphone or sound system?. Whatever technology you use, make sure you test it the day before and then again an hour before the meeting start time. Also, ensure you have a back-up plan when something goes wrong with your technical equipment. Yes, it happens to the best of us!

5. What Traditional Equipment Is Needed?

We forget about this category in today's technical age. Will you need items such as a white board, flip chart, markers, erasers, extra pens or notepad paper?

6. What Type Of Refreshments Are Needed?

Depending on the time and length of the meeting, it is always a good idea to have appropriate food and drink available.. Keep the snacks and drinks healthy, simple and light. Make the snacks available before the meeting starts.

Do Your Homework

Shooting from the hip will always end in failure. You need to treat every meeting like it is the most important of your life. You need to be prepared. When you are prepared, you elevate your stature in the eyes of the meeting participants and you are more likely to achieve all your objectives. To be on top of your game and have everything in place, engage in the following activities prior to the meeting:

- Collect and review all relevant data, reports and material.
- Distribute materials and reports beforehand to all participants.
- Distribute the agenda a week before the meeting date. The agenda, described earlier will explain the meeting purpose to the participants and provide the expected outcome, roles of the participant, topics and schedule.
- Talk to participants about their expectations and opinions in order to grasp an understanding of their personal agendas and concerns.
- Encourage participants to be prepared before the meeting.

My Top Book Recommendations

If you would like to research this topic in more detail, I highly recommend the following books.

- The Complete Idiot's Guide to Meeting & Event Planning, 2nd Edition, by Robin E. Craven, Lynn Johnson Golabowski, ISBN-13: 978-1592574629

- Successful Meetings: How to Plan, Prepare, and Execute Top-Notch Business Meetings, by Shri Henkel, ISBN-13: 978-0910627917

- Plan and Conduct Effective Meetings: 24 Steps to Generate Meaningful Results, by Barbara J Streibel, ISBN-13: 978-0071498319

What will you learn next?

In the next chapter we focus on how you can become a Master Meeting Facilitator, making your meetings more effective, efficient and downright fun.

7. The Master Meeting Facilitator

Meetings are one key element of your business day. They can dramatically move your business forward or hold it back. Unfortunately, it feels like you spend most of your day in meetings that seem, and often are, a complete waste of time. Those who run effective meetings not only know when to meet, they also know "how" to meet. Let's explore how you can become a Master Meeting Facilitator, making your meetings more effective, efficient and downright fun.

In this chapter you will learn:
- 12 key meeting facilitation techniques that top performers use
- 6 conflict resolution tips to get your meeting back on track
- 4 steps to follow when creating quality meeting minutes
- 7 critical sections included in quality meeting minutes

Why is Chaos the Norm?

"Free-For-All" is the term my clients use most often when they discuss meeting experiences. I'm sure you have lived through many meetings that would qualify for this title and agree that it is impossible to accomplish anything. These meetings have similar characteristics that include: no clear meeting objectives or expected outcome, no clear meeting leader, very loud and disruptive participants, many distractions, overbearing personalities, and irrelevant topics. I'm sure you can add many more items to the list.

If you want to become a top performer, you will need to overcome what 95% of the business professionals have not been able to do. You need to become a "Master Meeting Facilitator". In the previous chapter you learned how to organize and prepare for your meeting. Now, we will look at a few simple steps that will keep your meetings focused and on track to achieve your meeting purpose and expected outcome. By following these simple steps, you will stand out above others, providing your clients with something rarely seen, an effective meeting that achieves real results.

Let's examine how a Master Meeting Facilitator leads a meeting.

Start Your Meeting on Time

Always, always, always start a meeting on time. When a meeting is scheduled to start at 9:00am, don't start at 8:55 a.m. or 9:05 a.m. Start at exactly 9:00 a.m. Starting early, as meeting participants are still arriving, is simply unprofessional. Starting late is just as bad. As the old saying goes, "time is money". If you are holding a meeting, it must be very important to the business and everybody must realize they need to be ready at the appropriate start time. Master meeting facilitators always start the meeting on time, no matter what.

Clients frequently ask, "What should I do when meeting participants arrive five minutes late and miss the beginning of the meeting?" The answer is very simple. Keep moving forward through your agenda.

Don't reward tardiness by restarting the meeting. This rewards bad behavior and wastes precious time for everyone else. After the first few meetings, everybody will realize they need to be in their seats before the meeting start time.

Begin Your Meeting with Introductions

Allow time at the beginning of each meeting to introduce new participants or guests. This is a very professional way to introduce new members to the group and help facilitate camaraderie between participants. If there is time before the meeting, casually introduce new members to other participants. At the beginning of the meeting, you can introduce each member yourself or ask him or her to stand and provide his or her own introduction.

When giving an introduction, include:
- His or her name, title and company
- Role he or she will take during the meeting
- Brief background on his or her qualifications and reason for attending

Set the Tone With a Meeting Kickoff

After you make the brief introductions, you want to set the meeting tone by getting everybody on the same page. You want to prepare the participants for the work ahead. A majority of today's meetings jump right into the primary meeting topic. You are going to be different. Even if your client did not review the agenda that you sent out in advance, this portion of the meeting will get everyone up to speed quickly. You will stand out above others by following this approach and will avoid most of the problems that turn meetings into horrific nightmares.

During the meeting kickoff you should review the:
- meeting purpose;
- expected outcome of the meeting;
- participant roles

- agenda items and schedule;
- meeting ground rules

Covering the abovementioned points establishes the ground rules for the meeting. It is imperative to establish a set of behaviors and principles that participants agree on to ensure an effective meeting.

Ground rules

Note that all participants should agree to these ground rules.

- Agree on the agenda items
- Keep on schedule
- Agree on how to handle conflicts
- Ensure that everyone freely participates in the discussions
- Determine how and who will make the final decisions
- Implement time limits for solving challenges and making decisions
- Determine how and when you will complete meeting action items
- Agree on how and when you may table items for a later time

If you keep these ground rules simple and articulate them clearly, you can be assured that they will foster greater participation and will enhance the effectiveness of your meeting.

Review Previous Action Items

How many meetings do you attend where you are unaware of why it has been called? Do you ever attend meetings where management discusses open issues and actions and then those items disappear never to be discussed again?. In this section of the meeting it is important to get all participants up to speed on the latest developments.

During this section, you should provide a summary:
- on the topic background that led to this meeting. Do this for the first meeting on a topic.
- of previously held meetings and offline conversations concerning the topic. This should be a very short summary.
- status on the previous meeting issues and action items. Review the results of those items or if not completed, where they are in the process of being resolved. Ask the owners of the action items to provide clarification or details as necessary.

At this point, the participants should now be up to speed on the latest developments and will be ready to proceed through the primary topics you will cover in the meeting.

Keep Your Meeting Focused

Don't allow meeting participants to digress on irrelevant topics. When discussing each topic, keep track of the items you are discussing and the time allocated to them. Document key points, comments and issues related to the topic on a flip chart or white board under the topic name. This helps all meeting participants stay focused. If you feel someone is introducing an irrelevant item, ask the group to table that item for now. They can discuss it "offline" or in another meeting. Keep a list of these topics on a separate flip chart.

Don't let the discussions linger just because time remains for the topic. When you feel you have reached an agreement, summarize it for the meeting participants and then ask to move on to the next topic.

By following these tips, you will keep your meeting participants focused on the topic at hand and keep the meeting running on schedule.

Get Everyone to Participate

All points of view are valuable. Depending on the meeting topic, some viewpoints will be more valuable than others. Depending on the purpose of the meeting, it might make sense to have senior meeting participants begin the discussions. If it is important to hear everybody's opinion, you might ask the senior meeting participants to wait until everybody provides input. This will encourage junior participants to open up during the meeting.

Watch and listen for all participants who want to provide input during a particular discussion but might be hesitant to join in. Help involve them by saying, "Let's get some input from Rick and then Judy."

A few additional points will help you get full participation:
- Ask for feedback. For example, "Have we left anything out?"
- Ask someone to play devil's advocate. Challenge the assumptions and decisions you are posing.
- When your meeting has a large number of participants, divide the group into smaller sub-groups. After a period of time, instruct the sub-groups to report back to the main group.

New ideas and solutions can come from the most unlikely meeting participants. Everybody's input is important and should be treated with respect.

Meeting Leaders Must Lead

Meeting leaders are in a position to inspire greatness or create a disaster. Your actions create a meeting atmosphere that will encourage meeting participants to contribute or drive them into complete silence and indifference.

As the leader, follow these guidelines to inspire greatness:

- Control participants who are dominating the discussion or interrupting others.
- Create the opportunity for quiet participants to contribute their views.
- Document input and decisions on a flip chart. Reference this information to highlight areas of agreement to prevent participants from reopening issues.
- Don't dominate the entire discussion. You're leading, not dictating.
- Intervene if meeting participants are criticizing the opinions of others. Don't allow it to continue.
- Make positive and encouraging comments about participants' opinions.
- Remain in control at all times. Keep your emotions in check.

Effectively Handling Meeting Conflict

Handling conflict in your meeting will become one of your greatest assets. We all expect a meeting to run smoothly. We normally are not prepared to handle disruptions. When major conflicts arise, most professionals are caught off guard and usually do not handle the situation properly. You will be different. A conflict may develop during debates on how best to solve a challenge, or when discussions avoid the root cause of a problem, or at the point where we must make a decision. Yes, it can get so bad that it degenerates into an all out brawl, including the punches. starts.

None of these situations will cause you to lose control if you are prepared to handle them beforehand with the following conflict analysis and resolution tips.

Conflict Analysis:
A top performer pays close attention to what the meeting participants are saying, both verbally and non-verbally. The words said the participant conveys will tell you half the story. The participant's body language, eye contact, facials expressions and tone of voice

will tell you what he or she is really feeling about a topic or the points you are making. For example, Ted is normally a warm and open person but he now has his arms tightly folded across his chest and is looking down at the table. This indicates that he may be holding back critical comments that you and the group need to hear.

Based on your conflict analysis, the following conflict resolution tips will help you become proactive in refocusing the meeting and avoiding major conflicts.

Conflict Resolution Tips:

1. When participants become overly emotional:
- ask open ended questions that probe further into a topic to uncover underlying personal issues;
- ask participants who are not able to control their tempers to deal with their emotions outside;
- encourage everyone not to evaluate ideas too quickly;
- encourage everyone to keep comments positive and constructive;
- focus on the substance, not the personal style of the individual participant;
- inform everyone that it is okay to be passionate about a topic as long as it does not distract from the meeting purpose and objectives;
- re-address the behavior guidelines that you agreed upon in the meeting kickoff;
- ask them to leave the meeting if they are becoming too disruptive (worse case scenario).

2. When participants repeat the same points over and over:
- keep track of ideas, solutions and concerns on a flip chart;
- point to the flip chart and say, "I believe we have that point here, is that correct?"

3. When participants are afraid to bring up a topic or idea:

- remind them that all opinions, options, ideas, concerns and issues are very important;
- make it clear that the policy is *not* to "kill the messenger";
- reinforce the point that controversial discussions are often the key for getting the best solution;
- thank a participant for bringing up a different view point.

4. When all participants become quiet:

- take a quick look around at the body language and facial expressions which might tell the story;
- ask the group if you were unclear and if they require additional information on the topic;
- don't speak immediately; let the silence linger for a few moments to see if someone jumps in to speak.

5. When participants are stuck on one point:

- determine the cause of the roadblock. Are they lacking information or need clarification on specific items?
- point out the purpose and expected outcome for the meeting;
- request a quick break to get everybody to relax. Then revisit the topic on their return;
- suggest that you move the topic later in the agenda;
- propose that you table the topic for another meeting or handle it " offline".

6. When a participant is dominating the meeting:

- call on other participants to obtain their input;
- ask him or her to allow the other participant to finish his or her thought before providing additional input.
- ask the meeting participant to write down his or her thoughts during the break and at the appropriate time invite him or her to review those thoughts with the group.

- request a participant leave the meeting when they become completely out of control.

Remember, you are a top performer and leader. Use those skills to help the group participants to achieve the meeting purpose, objectives and expected outcome.

Summarize Accomplishments with a Meeting Recap

At the end of the meeting you want some time set aside to review what you accomplished. This portion of the meeting is critical. It solidifies the decisions and agreements that you and the participants made. The recap also provides an executive summary for your meeting minutes which we will describe later.

Here are a few items that you should cover during the meeting recap:
- Summarize what was accomplished.
- Summarize open issues and action items. Identify the owner of each item and when responses are due back to the team.
- Provide a general summary on the outcome of the meeting. Point out positive aspects on how you ran the meeting and, how the participants engaged in the discussions..
- Ask the participants to provide feedback on what you could do to improve the next meeting.

Confirm Your Next Steps

Never end a meeting without finalizing what will happen next. Once again, make this topic an agenda item. Schedule the next meeting date. If there are multiple meetings in the future, confirm the next meeting and attempt to schedule as many as possible in advance. If you are involved in a project or sales process, outline the next steps in the process and commit to milestone dates. End your meeting by thanking everyone for participating.

Ending Your Meeting On Time

Everyone has a busy schedule and must deal with back-to-back meetings. Master meeting facilitators always keep the meeting on track and end on time. They make a commitment to themselves and the meeting participants to never overrun the stated time.

To accomplish this, you must:
- keep track of the meeting time. Assign a timekeeper to keep the meeting on track using the agenda schedule;
- remind the participants of the time remaining and topics you will cover;
- gain agreement to move items to another meeting if time is running out;
- gain agreement to run overtime on critical items that you must discuss at this particular meeting.

Time is a valuable commodity. Don't waste it.

Follow-up Quickly with Meeting Minutes

It is amazing how quickly some participants forget the important discussions and decisions only hours after leaving a meeting. How about those meeting participants who agree to take ownership of action items and never follow through? This has delayed many decisions in the past and will continue to do so unless you, as a top performer, take action. The most effective tool to ensure meeting success after the meeting, is to provide participants with a written meeting summary.. The most common term for this is "Meeting Minutes".

Your meeting minutes will differ from the normal discussion and decisions list. . You will provide a meeting summary unlike anything your client has ever received. This simple action gives the participant a sense of accomplishment. They are able to see in writing solid meeting results which will provide a direction moving forward.

The quicker you deliver meeting minutes to participants, the better. Top performers will send out meeting minutes within 24 hours. Yes, within one day, all participants and those not in attendance should receive a copy .

Preparing Your Minutes
Follow these steps to develop high quality meeting minutes:

1. Take good notes during the meeting
Many top performers have found that the best meeting minutes result when a participant is assigned responsibility for taking notes. We refer to this person as the scribe. This participant's primary role is to concentrate on what is being said and to document that information. Now, of course, you will not have a scribe for all your meetings. All is not lost. You too, can follow these steps to produce effective meeting minutes.

2. Concentrate on the 3 W's
Pay special attention to "what", "who" and "when" as you are taking meeting notes.

- **What** decisions, alternatives, action items, steps, or issues are you discussing?
- **Who** is the person responsible for resolving issues and action items?
- **When** are the items due? Every action must have a corresponding due date.

3. Take notes
A notepad or a flip chart are the most common tools we use to take meeting notes. Many professionals also use white boards and brown paper taped to the walls. My personal favorite is the laptop computer. Typing notes directly into a meeting minutes form will save you valuable time when you prepare your meeting minutes. Using this method often saves me one to two hours a day. Use whatever method works best for you.

4. Collect meeting notes from others

Ask other participants in the meeting to copy you on their notes. You will find valuable information and view points based on the interpretations of others. Combine this information with your notes.

What's included in the Meeting Minutes?

The best meeting minutes are organized in sections starting with the overview and ending with the detail action items. They are also short and concise.. You are not writing a book. Keep your focus on the meeting goals, objectives, expected outcome and the three W's when you develop your meeting minutes document. For most meetings, the entire minutes package will be one to three pages maximum.

Let's look at the sections you should include.

1. Meeting Agenda

Placing the original meeting agenda as the first page of your meeting minutes serves many purposes. This serves as a review of the meeting purpose and expected outcome. It recaps the participant's role in attending the meeting. Finally, it provides an outline of previously covered topics. This should take about ten seconds to copy and paste right into your meeting minutes.

2. Meeting Results – Executive Summary

Provide a short summary of the meeting. Specifically address the meeting results and how they relate to the meeting purpose and expected outcome. This should be short, concise and written in simple, non-technical language. Many executives do not have time to read the whole document and will only read this summary. Make sure the meeting results are in this section.

3. Previous Issue and Action Item Updates

Provide an updated list of the issues and action items from prior meetings. You can also copy this from the meeting agenda. Make the necessary updates to item owners, due dates and the status of those items. This section will provide a quick summary on how the team has progressed.

4. Discussion
This section includes details from the meeting. As we discussed before, use your notes, the scribe's and other participants notes to develop a detailed list of what you discussed during the meeting. Organize the material to follow the topics on the agenda. There are two primary styles for writing this section 1) bullet points and 2) paragraph form. Many top performers and I, as well as our clients, prefer the bullet point method. You need to determine what works best for your client.

Include the following in your discussion points:
- Highlight the key discussion topics.
- Record the decisions.
- Describe the key challenges, problems or issues.
- List alternative solutions.
- Jot down pros and cons for the alternative solutions you discussed.
- Bullet point the criteria for making a decision.
- Make note of what actions you will need to take in the future.
- Future expected outcomes

5. Issues to Investigate
List the new issues you have identified during the meeting. Provide a description, the participant who owns the issue and the due date for a resolution. By documenting this, the participants will have a responsibility and obligation to resolve the issue for the team.

6. Action Items
List the action items and next steps that you identified in the meeting. As with new issues, provide a description of the action item, the participant who owns the action and the due date for completion.

7. Next Meeting

Last, but not least, document the date for the next meeting and the topics for discussion. This will give everyone a head start to prepare for the meeting. Be as detailed as possible, including; date, time, location, attendees, meeting name, meeting purpose, expected outcome, draft agenda and participant roles. You may not be able to provide all this information, but give it your best shot. When you can, your clients will be very impressed.

My Top Book Recommendations

If you would like to research this topic in more detail, I highly recommend the following books.

- Meeting Excellence: 33 Tools to Lead Meetings That Get Results, by Glenn M. Parker, Robert Hoffman, ISBN-13: 978-0787982812

- Death by Meeting: A Leadership Fable...About Solving the Most Painful Problem in Business, by Patrick M. Lencioni, ISBN-13: 978-0787968052

- The Secrets of Facilitation: The S.M.A.R.T. Guide to Getting Results With Groups, by Michael Wilkinson, ISBN-13: 978-0787975784

What will you learn next?

In the next chapter we focus on how using the right words and stories when delivering your ideas and recommendations will convince your client that you have the solution they need.

8. Using the Most Effective Words and Stories

Essential to being an effective top performer is paying attention to the language you use and how you use it. You can express yourself in many ways.. Each client will receive you differently. It may be challenging for you to convey your vast knowledge to a less informed or less knowledgeable client. Often, this lack of knowing how to communicate can lead to misunderstandings which can upset a client. Using the right words and stories when delivering your ideas and recommendations will convince your client that you have the solution he or she needs.

In this chapter you will learn:
- □ 4 personality styles and how best to work with each
- □ 10 tips for developing effective business stories
- □ How to use the right words to make your point
- □ 3 step process for selecting the right words and knowing those to avoid
- □ How to develop a client dictionary

Understand Your Clients Personality

Ignoring your client's personality while communicating verbally or in writing can have severe consequences. A personality style clash with an important client can bring the relationship to an abrupt finish. It's that simple. How can this happen? Most professionals tend to communicate in a way that matches their own personality, not the client's. While this is natural for you, the client's personality might not react well to your communication style.

Have you ever lost a client and could not pinpoint exactly why? When your manager or partner asked what happened, your response was something like this: "He just doesn't like me" or "There is something wrong with him. We didn't get along from the beginning" or "He must have a serious personal problem because this solution was perfect for them".

After seeing hundreds of these situations with clients, it is very clear what happens. The professional and client have two different personality styles that clash. Neither one tries to understand the other or, communicate in a manner that would allow the other to feel most comfortable.

Your goal as a top performer is to understand the four different personality styles. Then, determine your style and which style is dominant in your client. Once you have this understanding, you need to adjust your communication methods to match the style of your client. This will make him or her feel more comfortable with you, your ideas and recommendations.

1. The Aggressive Personality
This client tends to keeps his or her emotions inside. During conversations he or she tends to dominate and tell you what needs done. They ask few questions. You find this personality style mainly in leadership positions like a business executive, entrepreneur, or plant manager.

Primary Characteristics:
- Biggest ego in the room
- Direct and to the point
- Brief
- Loves authority
- Delegates
- Very decisive
- Competitive personally and professionally
- Driven to succeed
- Tough skinned
- Will bend or break rules if needed

2. The Analytical Personality

This client tends to keep his or her emotions inside. He or she acts like an introvert. During conversations he or she will ask many questions. You find this personality style mainly in project managers, planners, accountants, engineers, scientists, programmers and researchers.

Primary Characteristics:
- Detail oriented
- Wants facts, figures, spreadsheets and charts
- Prefers to work alone
- Deliberate in the action they take
- Critical of others but does not accept criticism well
- Expects work to be accurate and timely
- Perfectionist
- Excellent problem solver
- Follows rules by the book

3. The Outgoing Personality

This client tends to display his or her emotions openly. He or she loves to talk. He or she doesn't ask many questions during conversations and tends to tell many stories. You find this personality style mainly in clients working in communications, sales, marketing and public relations.

Primary Characteristics:
- Works well with others
- Wants to be part of a team
- Likes attention focused on them
- First to volunteer
- Motivates and inspires
- Weak on follow-up

4. The Nurturing Personality

This client tends to easily share his or her feelings. During conversations he or she will ask many questions. He or she seems easy going and nice to be around. You find this personality style mainly in clients working in customer service, counseling, human resources, administration and support.

Primary Characteristics:
- Great listeners
- Helpful
- Stays in the background
- Personal relationships are very important
- Avoids high pressure situations
- Will not choose sides when confronted
- Avoids making decisions

How to Interact with Different Personalities

It is amazing how you can quickly pinpoint a personality style once you understand the four different personalities. First, you need to determine which is your dominant style. Review the different characteristics and honestly settle on which is your most dominant style. Next, think about your previous client meetings and establish which characteristics best match your client.

At this point you might ask, " Why do I need to understand my own personality style?" The quick answer is: certain styles clash and others get along better.

For example:
- People with the same personality styles do not always work well together.
- Analytical and aggressive personalities have a hard time getting along.
- Outgoing and nurturing personalities have a difficulty getting along.
- Analytical and nurturing personalities work well together.
- Aggressive and outgoing personalities work well together

When communicating with clients, you need to understand the different characteristics and be sensitive to your client's personality style. Let's take a look at how you can better communicate with the different personality styles.

Aggressive Personality
- Don't challenge his or her authority
- Focus on helping him or her succeed
- Get to your point quickly
- Keep briefings as short as possible
- Leave your ego at home
- Let him or her control the conversation

Analytical Personality
- Avoid pushing collaborative work teams
- Deliver work on time
- Don't ask him or her to break the rules
- Double check and verify all work
- Provide detail information
- Use more statistics and charts

Outgoing Personality
- Don't ask him or her to perform detail analysis
- Focus on meeting his or her needs
- Focus on positive topics
- Have him or her work on collaborative teams
- Use him or her to motivate others

Nurturing Personality
- Build a personal relationship
- Don't ask him or her to lead initiative
- Don't ask him or her to make a critical decision
- Have him or her work on collaborative teams
- Talk through solution alternatives
- Use as a mediator

Respect your client's personality style. Don't try to force your style onto them or change his or hers. If you follow these simple rules, you will be well on your way to becoming a top performer.

Tell Your Client a Business Story

Visual images help your clients better understand and accept your ideas and recommendations. Like your grandfathers storytelling, a business story relates images and anecdotes so your client can visualize the information you present. When used correctly, your client will see you as a top performer instead of just another business professional.

Your business story goal is to communicate your ideas and recommendations by relating business anecdotes and other client successes so the client can experience your successful solution. A business story uses all your client's senses. This enables your client to feel more comfortable and willing to accept your ideas.

Why a Business Story Works

You develop emotional attachment between you and your client because business stories are a personal communication method. They build a bond and understanding between individuals. To illustrate this point, I want to tell you a personal story that illustrates the effectiveness of a story.

Last year I was looking for a new sport utility vehicle or van for my family. I decided one day to visit dealerships and look at my top five choices. Four dealers asked me the standard questions such as: How much do you want to pay? What color do you prefer?. Next they would hand me brochures and elaborate on the great features for that model. The managers and salesman were friendly, courteous, and answered my questions. But, after visiting four dealerships, I felt I knew as much as I did after researching those vehicles on the internet.

Something different happened at the fifth dealer. Greeting me at the door was Tom. This salesman began asking me questions about what I wanted from a new vehicle. He did not just ask me the specific feature and price questions. After sitting down over a coffee telling him my needs for the perfect vehicle, he conveyed to me his personal experiences with the Honda Pilot he purchased a year ago. Tom told me stories about taking the Pilot on camping trips, taking his grandkids' soccer team out after games and how the car handled through the crowded downtown streets during rush hour. At one point, he asked another customer, Ruth, who was waiting on an oil change, to come over and tell me about her experience driving her Honda Pilot cross country. After hearing these stories for 20 minutes, I felt like I had all these experiences myself. I could see, hear, smell and feel driving this SUV. I was now emotionally attached and knew this was the right vehicle for me.

I am sure you have experienced the same in a business or personal situation. Often, a good story is more effective than any other communication.

Why is it effective?

- It inspires the client to accept your recommendations based on a personal connection.

- You describe your ideas, recommendations and value in a non-traditional manner that involves your client.

- You don't sound like everyone else they talk with on a daily basis.

- Clients can visualize success through another person's experience. Your client will feel more comfortable about implementing your solution.

How to Develop an Effective Business Story

Successful business stories, like many other effective tools, have a format and approach that will give you the best results. Follow these tips and techniques when developing a business story for your next client.

1. Write down the goal of your story. What is the primary message your want to communicate to your clients. For example: Customers are reducing inventory levels by as much as 57% after 8 months on our XYZ program.

2. Write down the top five key points you want to communicate. These are the top points in support of your message. For example: How did you reduce inventory? What investment did you need? What was the ROI? How did others engage in the program?

3. Give your story a unique title. Something that will help the client remember it over all the other information they process each day. For example, "The Cow" or "Refreshing the Herd".

4. The business story must be short and to the point. Keep it to under one written page or five minutes.

5. Include quotes and statistics as much as possible. These can come from other clients, industry experts, or research

groups. Third party confirmation is a very effective technique to increase acceptance of your story.

6. When developing a business story, keep it relevant to your client's challenges.

7. Use familiar words and phrases to your client's industry and job title. Your clients will be able to relate better to a story that uses language they understand.

8. Liven up your story. Use descriptive language that targets each of the five senses.

9. Make the story more personal. Use the first names of your clients when telling the story.

10. Practice, practice, practice. Write out your story and practice your delivery. You want your story to sound conversational. To achieve this, practice the story as much as possible.

Although telling a business story in person is the most effective, you can use the same points above to convey your story in direct mail pieces, articles, on the phone, or via web conferencing.

Example Business Story–Before

This example is a very weak value story. Unfortunately, many professionals believe this is a sound business story. The result is the client doesn't feel confident in the stated value that the storyteller delivered. The storyteller wanted to demonstrate why a previous client made the decision to do business with this consultant.

> Our service has delivered the results you desire. ABC Company had the same concerns last year. Once they performed a detailed analysis of the cost and benefits, they decided to sign a contract with us for this service.

Example Business Story–After

Let's take a look at a short, successful business story response. This is the type of business story your will hear from top performers.

> Twelve months ago, Brenda Phillips at ABC Company had the same concerns you have. Brenda is the CEO based in the New York City. She decided to have her team study our financial analysis to determine if the proposed value was valid or even possible.
>
> Brenda's team spent 30 days performing a thorough review of our analysis. After her team delivered their analysis, Brenda immediately phoned and said she wanted to go with us on this project. Brenda believed our service would increase sales by at least 30% which was 7% more than our conservative projections.
>
> We received a call from Brenda just a month ago and she said the service has worked out better than expected. They have already increased sales by more than 30% after the first six months.

Types of Business Stories

Cover your bases. Create a broad range of business stories that can be used at any point in the client relationship. The more areas you have covered, the more successful you will be in attaching emotions to your ideas and recommendations.

Here is a sample list of stories to develop for each product or service:
- Client success case studies
- Delivery objection story
- Firm size objection story
- How you are different
- Industry specific stories
- Large client story
- Long time client story
- New client story
- Payback story
- Price objection story
- Quality story
- Return on investment story
- Schedule objection story
- Small client story
- Staffing objection story
- Value story
- Who you are
- Why do this now?
- Why does the customer need you?
- Why you are so successful?

Using the Right Words To Make Your Point

To be an effective top performer it is crucial to pay attention to the language you use. There are many ways to express yourself and remember that each client will receive you differently. Maybe you don't know how to convey your knowledge to a client with lesser knowledge. Your job as a top performer is to help your client understand your ideas and recommendations in a language they understand and respect.

When talking with a client, you need to avoid defensiveness by paying careful attention to the words and phrasing you use. Here is a simple and effective secret. Talk with your clients as if they were your grandmother. That's right. Avoid using "hard" phrasing like, "You must do X". This will be met with emotional resistance and defensiveness. No one likes to be told what to do, even if you are right. If you were talking with your grandmother, you would rephrase this statement to something like this. "Let's talk through your options together. These are the options I see. Do you think there is anything else we should consider?" Phrasing your words in this manner creates a respectful dialogue that is key for successful advisers.

There are numerous phrasing examples that we can review. For example, take the phrase, "What are your problems?" This simple, yet challenging will put the client on the defensive. Instead, try, "What areas are most in need of improvement?" How about the phrase, "This is the best solution for you." ? Instead, try "My other clients have tried "X" for these reasons. Do you think this would apply here?"

The golden rule is to express yourself in a way that creates a dialogue the clients understands, respects and gets the feeling you are helping them.

Words to Use and Those to Avoid

How do you know which words to use and which ones to avoid? Where do we begin? Follow this step-by-step process for collecting the words and phrases to avoid and those you should use when talking with clients.

1. List words you use in your own company
Start by collecting a list of words that people in your company use.. Avoid these words when you talk with a client.

2. Read the trade publications that are relevant to your clients
These can be industry, business unit or job title specific. If your client is a mass merchandise retailer you might pick up the magazine *Chain Store* Another option is to look at your clients business unit. If your client is a retail IT executive, you might read through the magazine *RIS – Retail Information Systems* for retail specific IT terminology or *Computer World* for general IT terminology. Another option is to look at your client's job title.

What trade magazines do they read? A CFO might read *CFO* or a project manager would most likely read *PM Network*

3. List key words and phrases used by trade publications

While reading the client trade publications, make a list of often used unique industry terms and concepts. These are the words and phrases you need when talking with your clients.

Let's take a quick look at an example list of general words to avoid and those to use when talking with clients.

Words to avoid

These make you sound like your selling, not helping a client. Do these resemble the language that people in your company use?

- Appointment
- Company
- Contract
- Deal
- Demo
- Invoice
- Order
- Pilot
- Presentation
- Price
- Proof of Concept
- Proposal
- Purchase Order
- Quota
- Request For Proposal
- Sales
- Software
- Technology

Negative words to avoid

- Anxious
- Disappoint
- Failure
- Fear

- Fearful
- Frightened
- Impatient
- Insecure
- Irritate
- Maybe
- Overload
- Overwhelm
- Perhaps
- Possibly
- Reject
- Sometimes
- Stress
- Stupid

Client language you should use

These are the words your client uses most frequently. By using these words, your client will view you as a peer or partner.

- Briefing
- Challenges
- Chat
- Client
- Competitive Advantage
- Discuss
- Engage
- Investment
- Market Share
- Meeting
- Partner
- Performance
- Productivity
- Return on Investment
- Scorecard
- Strategic
- Tactical
- Value
- Workshop

Positive words that promote enthusiasm and excitement
- Absolutely
- Better than
- Brilliant
- Captivating
- Compelling
- Confident
- Ecstatic
- Empowered
- Energized
- Excellent
- Excited
- Extraordinary
- Fabulous
- Fantastic
- Focused
- Great
- Invincible
- Now
- Passionate
- Perfect
- Superb
- Unstoppable
- Vibrant
- Winner

Create a Client Dictionary

You scare clients away when you use words or phrases that make you sound like an outsider. If your goal is to communicate a message of a top performer and if you want the client to view you like a partner, you need to use the client's language. The best way to accomplish this is to organize a client dictionary. A client dictionary is a list of key words and phrases that your clients use when conducting business. This is your client's vocabulary.

Why use the client's vocabulary and not your own? By using familiar words and phrases, you send a message that you are just like him or her. He or she will be more willing to accept you, your ideas and recommendations. Otherwise you will sound like every other consultant or sales professional that wastes time everyday and you will limit your likelihood for success.

Organizing Your Client Dictionary

You need to organize your client key words and phrases in a manner that is easily accessible and relevant to your specific client. The best way is to organize your client dictionary by industry verticals, business units, functional areas, and job titles.

Below is a partial client dictionary index used by Kelly, a top management consultant.

Industries
- Banking
- Financial Services
- Healthcare
- Manufacturing
- Retail
- Technology

Business Units
- Consumer Division
- Corporate Division
- Internet Division
- Government Division
- North America Division

Functional Areas
- Distribution
- Finance
- Human Resources
- Information Technology

- Marketing
- Purchasing
- Sales

Job Title
- Analyst
- CEO
- CFO
- CIO
- COO
- Manager
- Project Manager

Organizing your material in this manner provides quick access to the proper words and phrases for you to use with your client the next time you meet. Your client will view you as a partner and peer instead of a consultant and salesperson.

My Top Book Recommendations
If you would like to research this topic in more detail, I highly recommend the following books.

- All Marketers Are Liars: The Power of Telling Authentic Stories in a Low-Trust World, by Seth Godin, ISBN-13: 978-1591841005

- The Story Factor (2nd Revised Edition), by Annette Simmons, Doug Lipman, ISBN-13: 978-0465078073

- The Leader's Guide to Storytelling: Mastering the Art and Discipline of Business Narrative, by Stephen Denning, ISBN-13: 978-0787976750

What will you learn next?

In the next chapter we focus on how you can turn two overlooked communication methods into big opportunities for your business and career.

9. The Most Overlooked Written Communication

How many times have you talked with a client about an important matter and the next day you could not remember vital pieces of information to move forward with your work? Maybe you couldn't remember a key action item, the name of an analyst you were supposed to call, or worse yet, the client's core problem. Sometimes it's the little things that make a difference in your business and career. Top performers specialize in doing the little things right. A business journal and thank you note are two little items that can turn an average performer into a top performer.

In this chapter you will learn:
- ☐ 8 key pieces of information in a business journal
- ☐ 2 primary journal methods used by top performers
- ☐ 11 critical items top performers keep in their business journal
- ☐ 4 critical tips when sending a thank you note

Goldmine Found in Keeping
a Business Journal

Top performers are always knowledgeable of a broad range of clients, industries and specialty areas. How do they do that? Do they have a higher IQ or a better memory? No, they have found a secret-- keeping a business journal.

What is a business journal? A business journal is a log that top performers use to document discussions with clients, industry experts, product and service gurus. It also tracks what you have worked on and what you need to focus on in the future. A business journal may also track critical problems, brainstorming ideas, people to contact and new process improvements. The benefits to a business journal are infinite. Fast-paced business people tend to overlook this simple, obvious, but effective communication tool.

You do not use most of your life-long knowledge due to the access limitations of our memory and the lack of recorded information. If somebody asked you for the details of a meeting held nine months ago with a CEO regarding next year's strategies, would you be able to recall the specifics of the discussion? Most likely, no. If you did take notes, are they stuffed in a file or more likely, thrown away?

A business journal allows you to easily access past information that will make you a more effective top performer. The journal provides an easy way to access information when you need to recall:

- client details;
- industry information;
- solutions to challenges;
- what you accomplished;
- what partners accomplished;
- what your client accomplished;
- what you are currently working on;
- and anything else important to your business.

Starting Your Business Journal

First, you need to decide what you will use for your business journal. The variety of options include a notebook or electronic software. Let's explore the pros and cons of these two options. Both are fantastic tools and you will decide what to use based on your personal preference.

1. Leather Bound Notebooks
Professional looking and portable, a notebook and pen is the easiest way to get started. You can use a notebook anywhere and anytime. Many professionals use a spiral notebook or composition book for their journal. Yes, this is the cheapest way to go, but when sitting in front of clients these notebooks give the wrong impression. You do not want to convey a cheap, inexperienced and unprofessional impression. Spend a few extra dollars on a professional looking leather bound notebook. Major office supply stores sell quality leather bound notebooks at reasonable prices.

Searching a notebook for specific entries is the most common problem. Search ability of notebooks is not as simple as electronic journals, but you can make it easier by following a few tips. First, write key words about your entry at the top of the page. Second, you can create an index for that particular journal using the key words at the top of the page. This will take time to create, however it will be worth it when you need to research a hot topic.

2. Electronic Software
Faster access to large volumes of information is the primary benefit of electronic software. Have you ever tried to carry 15 year's worth of business journals on a plane? I didn't think so. Keeping an electronic journal is very easy for those comfortable with computers. Turn on the computer, open the software and start typing. Searching for information is as easy as typing in keywords in a search box and hitting the enter key. For those on the road or working at client locations, a notebook computer is a good choice. You can make entries into your journal while in the airport, on

the plane, sitting in the client's parking lot, or in your hotel. It is also becoming more common to take journal notes on a notebook computer while in client meetings. If you can type, this method is as easy as writing with a pen.

There are numerous ways to keep electronic journals on your computer, whether a desktop, notebook, or Palm-Top computer. The simplest and least expensive software to use is Windows Notebook. The second simplest and a little more expensive is word processing software like Microsoft Word. A more sophisticated alternative would be journaling software. There are many journaling products available, so it might be worth your while to search Google (http://www.google.com) or ZDNet (http://www.zdnet.com) and try out a few.

Information You Should Keep in Your Journal

What should you write in your journal? Everything and anything about your clients, industry, specialty, challenges, activities, thoughts and ideas! Keep as much or as little information as you wish. Keep in mind, the more details you include, the easier it will be to find the information you need when you are working on a critical challenge.

What do top performers write in their business journals?
- Solutions to company problems
- Solutions to client problems
- Your professional accomplishments
- Meeting minutes
- Phone or conference call notes
- Action item list
- Business contact information
- Client article notes
- Industry article and book notes
- Future business ideas
- Anything else that is important to you and your business

Your business journal is easy to start and simple to continue. It will take some time to get used to at first, but it is an easily learned habit.

Showing Genuine Gratitude with a Thank You

When we receive new client business, a verbal thank you is automatic. A verbal thank you is appropriate and necessary, but clients can perceive it as less than genuine because we automatically use this phrase. It becomes no different than saying good morning or commenting on the weather.

There are a variety of ways we can show gratitude other than a verbal thank you. Email notes are very popular. We can also present our clients with sports tickets, dinners, food baskets, pens, shirts, or golf balls to express thanks. Like a verbal thank you, these forms of gratitude are so common, many clients pay no attention. Also, with new corporate governance policies, these forms of gratitude may cause problems for the client or can be perceived as inducements or bribes to win over a customer.

If you want to stand out above everyone else, emulate the top performers. Send a hand written thank you note. A hand written note is personal, rarely done and shows the client he or she is important enough for you take the time to send a proper thank you. This form of thank you is the most underutilized and most appreciated form of gratitude.

Impact of The Hand Written Thank You

Carl, an IT executive for a large Midwest Insurance company finds the lack of thank you notes very disturbing. After my first introduction meeting with Carl last year, I sent him a note thanking him for his time. A few days later I received a card from Carl thanking me for the thank you note. How many times does this happen?

During our second meeting, Carl brought up the subject of gratitude. He pulled a small wooden, hand crafted box from his book shelf.

Within the box were fifteen hand written thank you notes that he received over the past two decades. "Dennis," he said, "I receive over twenty thank you gifts a week that I throw in a big box and donate to a charitable cause. It feels like others are trying to buy a relationship. As for thank you emails and phone calls, I don't feel any appreciation from them. This small box of hand written notes represents the handful of people I actually trust and look forward to a strong business relationship. Now let's discuss how we can move forward with our business relationship.

A hand written thank you will not get you the business by itself, but it will help in building a strong personal and business bond with your clients.

When Should You Send a Thank You?

Top performers send personal thank you notes after:

- any occasion where you feel the thank you notes would be appropriate;
- contract Renewal;
- first meeting;
- major meetings;
- new contract;
- opportunity for new business;
- professional events;
- referral.

4 Rules of Thank You Notes

When sending a hand written thank you note, top performers make it genuine. This is just another reason top performers retain clients for decades. To do it right, top performers follow four simple rules.

1. Send It Immediately
Send the thank you note within two days of the event.

2. Be Professional

Write your thank you note on quality stationery. Write with your best hand writing. Consider purchasing professionally printed stationary with your company logo and your name.

3. Be Brief and Precise

Keep your note to eighty words or less, six to eight sentences. Specifically note the event for which you are sending the thank you and explain why it was meaningful to you. For example:

Thank you for sending the referral to Mr. Smith at XYZ company. I appreciate your confidence in my services.

4. Be Consistent

Send a thank you note after all appropriate events. Don't become one of those who only sends them after you clinch a new contract.

Thank You Note Example

The following is a brief and precise thank you note example.

Marsha,

Thank you very much for the referral to Neil James at XYZ Corporation. I appreciate your confidence in my strategic planning services.

Please do not hesitate to call me if you need anything.

Best Regards,

Dennis Sommer

P.S. I look forward to seeing you at the Retail convention in Las Vegas.

My Top Book Recommendations
If you would like to research this topic in more detail, I highly recommend the following books.

- How to Say It: Choice Words, Phrases, Sentences, and Paragraphs for Every Situation, Revised Edition, by Rosalie Maggio, ISBN-13: 978-0735202344

What will you learn next?

In the next chapter we focus on how you can learn to write effective business documents that will inspire and motivate your clients into action.

10. Writing Memos and Reports That Make an Impact

If the written word is the primary vehicle for business communication, why do people ignore so many memos, reports, letters and emails? The simple fact is most professionals have poor writing skills. Poorly written communication can result in lost sales, project delays, upset clients, rejected budgets or worse. By learning the key elements of effective written communication, you will be able to inspire and motivate your clients into action every time you send them a document.

In this chapter you will learn:
- [ ] 5 most common problems with memos and reports today
- [ ] How to motivate your audience into action
- [ ] 4 questions to answer before you begin
- [ ] 5 key elements in a powerful business document

The #1 Communication Method

Mastering the art of memo writing might not seem that important in today's business world, but the fact is, memos still remain the primary form of written communication. Their primary purpose is to inform and persuade the reader. Written internally within your organization, the memo goal is to communicate strategies, meeting results, research recommendations and employee performance. Companies also write external memos to clients to communicate advice, make recommendations, suggest strategies and provide new offerings. Memos are particularly important when the readers are spread out across multiple locations. Also, in today's technological age, we send most memos electronically via email instead of hardcopy, thus making them easier and quicker to distribute.

If memos are the primary vehicle for business communication, why are so many memos ignored? The simple fact is, most professionals have poor memo writing skills. Poorly written memos can result in lost sales, projects delays, rejected budgets or worse. Take a look at the memos you receive this week. How many do you read entirely and then take a requested action? You may be shocked to discover that less than 20% of the memos will fit into this category. Now, if your clients are only taking action on less than 20% or your memos, this might explain why you are not having the success you desire.

Why Most Memos Don't Get Results

Rodney, a top consultant with a large global consulting firm was working at their premier client when he got the shock of his life. He arrived at the client location one day when the CEO asked to see him in his office. Upon arrival, the CEO got right down to business. Rodney, you're a brilliant guy, but your memos read like my ten year old son's email. As he threw down a stack of memos on the table, he continued to say that his team can't make sound business decisions based on meaningless memos. He continued, "If you can't provide us with sound, logical information written in a manner that we can understand, I will have to find someone else who can."

Like Rodney, most professionals have never learned how to write effective memos. Fortunately for Rodney, this encounter was just the scare he needed to start learning how top performers write memos that obtain results.

Let's take a look at the five most common problems found in memos today. Do your memos suffer from one or more of the following memo killers?

1. Not written for the reader.

Most memos are written from the writer's point of view, focusing on his or her interests. Eighty percent of memos fail to persuade and motivate readers because the author never addresses the reader's needs in the memo. Instead, the writer focuses on what he or she wants.

2. Filled with technical jargon.

Most professionals write like they talk. They include technical jargon that is second nature to them. This is especially true for computer technology and scientific research professionals. Unfortunately, readers of your memo can't make sound decisions when they don't understand what you have written. Technical jargon includes industry specific abbreviations like PMP, DASD, ITIL, and ERP. It also includes words or phrases that have multiple meanings, depending on your industry or department. Phrases like data warehousing and data mining will mean something different to each individual. Another example is the use of sports terms when writing about a business topic.

3. No clear message.

Many professionals fail to consider the purpose of their memos. Without a clear message, the reader will not know what to do with the information or will ignore the memo entirely. For example, if you receive a memo with the subject line "New Staff" and the memo informs that the company requires additional staff at X dollars but does not provide an explanation, then it is likely people will either file or delete the memo.

4. Poorly organized.

Structuring memos is a lost art. E-mail and word processors have made the creation of memos so easy we now rarely outline our thoughts in a coherent structure. Today, we open our e-mail, type in our thoughts as quickly as possible and hit the send button. The result is a memo containing our unfocused thoughts that rarely persuade our reader to take action.

5. Too much information.

More is not always better. Having the ability to cut-and-paste information from the internet and other documents, plus building tables and charts from computer software, we are now able to quickly pull together massive amounts of information. This has given professionals the ability to quickly create a memo of five pages or more. Unfortunately, most readers only have the attention span to read one page.

Let's take a look at an example of a typical memo sent by professionals today.

Before: A Poorly Written Memo

The purpose of this memo is to gain approval for the purchase of new notebook computers for the sales team. Put yourself in the reader's shoes. Based on this memo, would you approve the purchase of new notebook computers?

To: Richard Sampson
cc: James Pitcher
From: Samantha Johnson
Date: November 1, 2006

Subject: New Computers

Richard,

Your sales team needs new computers. The best option would be a notebook computer. More specifically, a new notebook computer from the Dell Latitude line. The Dell Latitude D410 notebook computer weighs 3.8 pounds, with a 12.1" XGA active matrix screen, is 1.25" thin, has an 80GB hard drive, a 2.00 GHz Intel Pentium Processor, has an integrated Intel ProWireless solution and allows up to 2.0 GB of SDRAM memory. The price is roughly $1,300.

Let me know if you think this is a good idea and we can move forward.

As he might have guessed, Richard ignored this memo. It was written from the sender's point of view, not the reader's. There was no clear message, it was poorly organized and filled with technical jargon was meaningless to the reader.

How Top Performers Motivate with a Memo

Purpose, focus, clarity and structure are critical factors when top performers write memos. Top performers realize that written communication, like memos, is very important. You must write every memo in a way that grabs the reader's attention and motivates him or her to take action. To do this, we break down the memo writing process into two separate steps. First, before writing or typing, you must plan and organize. Ask yourself four key questions to help find the purpose and focus of the memo. The second step is to structure the memo in a way that will grab the reader's attention and provide him or her with sound reasoning for why he or she should take your recommended action or accept your point of view.

Let's start by examining what top performers do before starting a memo.

Four Questions to Answer Before You Begin

There are four key questions you must answer before starting any successful memo. They are:

1. Who are the readers?
Answering this question helps you frame your memo from the client's perspective. Tailor your communication to the reader, his or her background items of interest to them. Place yourself in the reader's shoes. Understand what he or she wants or needs to hear. For example, the CEO of a large organization would have interest in information that solved strategic challenges. At the other end of the spectrum, a line manager would be most interested in information to increase productivity or reduce workload.

2. What is the primary message?
Most professionals don't understand or think about a memo's key message or purpose. They just start writing. You need to ask yourself, "What is the one key piece of information that you want your reader to remember?" Top performers understand that a memo must focus on one key primary message. This will define your purpose and objective. Everything else in the memo will then support your primary message.

3. How should I send it?
What format should you use when sending a memo? Should it be sent via email, attached Word document, printed hardcopy or printed hardcopy on letterhead paper? Your should determine your format based on the importance of your memo and reader.

4. How can I keep it simple and to the point?
Often professionals have a tendency to over explain, throw in technical jargon and try to be too helpful. Top performers have mastered the art of creating a memo that is less than one page. You

need to keep focused on the primary message and what the reader needs to know to make a decision. Remember, it's quality not quantity that counts. Paragraphs can be one sentence long. Bullet points work well to emphasize your key points. Avoiding technical jargon helps all readers easily understand your information. For those memos that require supporting documentation like charts and financial spreadsheets, you can attach those to your memo in a separate document marked "Supporting information."

After answering the four questions above, you are now ready to move to the next step- actual creation of your memo.

How to Structure a Powerful Memo

Like a great article or presentation, a powerful memo must grab the reader's attention, motivate them to continue reading and inspire them to take action once read. The best way to make this happen is to structure your memo in a way that top performers have found to be most successful. There are five key elements in powerful memos.

1. Subject Line

The subject line of your memo is equivalent to a newspaper or magazine article headline. This is probably the most important sentence within your memo. You must immediately catch the reader's attention and motivate him or her to read your memo. The subject should be your memo's punch line. It should tell the reader how they will personally or professionally benefit from the information below. Which memo would you be more interested in reading, a memo with a subject line stating "New Software Recommended" or "New Software That Will Increase Sales Revenue 31% In 90 Days"?

2. Purpose

Successful memos include a statement that describes the key message and action the reader must take from the reader's point of view. If you do not state the memo's purpose, your reader will not understand why this information is important to them and will most likely not take the action that you desire. The purpose statement should take over where the subject line left off, enticing the reader to continue. For example, "Purpose: Review how the purchase of new sales software will increase sales revenue and client satisfaction".

3. Address the Challenges

You must ask yourself, "What problem are we trying to solve for the reader?" "What goals and objectives are most important to them?" Does the purpose of your memo affect the reader in a positive way, resolving their primary issues, problems or challenges? What is the reader getting out of this? For example, the proposed new sales software will increase sales revenue, which is in support of the CEOs number one strategic priority of increasing company growth by 50%. Therefore, if the CEO is the primary reader of this memo, state under "challenges addressed" how this memo will help the CEO achieve his or her company's growth goal.

4. Body – Supportive Main Points

Concentrate and focus on the three most important facts or ideas in support of your memo's purpose. For each of your main points, clarify your position in a simple, to- the- point manner. Emphasize key facts. Use statistics, testimonies, stories, anecdotes, research facts and visual aids which support your position. I find that bolding these key points is very effective in catching the reader's attention.

5. Recommendation

We rarely use recommendations in our memos, but they can be very effective. Include a recommendation section in your memos. The end of your memo is your final opportunity to convey your message, main points and reinforce the purpose of the memo. Your final statement should be a knockout punch that will persuade and motivate your reader to take the action you desire.

Now you are ready to put everything together. Let's examine how we transformed a bad memo into a very powerful and persuasive memo.

After: A Memo That Persuades

A well planned and structured memo is simple and to the point, addresses the readers key challenges, summarizes how they will overcome these challenges and shows the value of the recommended solution.

Let's take a look at an example memo, written by a top performing adviser. We have transformed the "before" memo into a very powerful, attention grabbing and motivating communication vehicle using the memo writing techniques of top performers.

To: Richard Sampson
cc: James Pitcher
From: Samantha Johnson
Date: November 1, 2005

Subject: New technology that will increase sales revenue and client satisfaction.

Purpose
To review how replacing desktop computers with new notebook computers will help you increase sales revenue, shorten your sales cycle and improve client satisfaction.

Challenges Addressed
Two of your corporate priorities this year include improving sales revenue by 17% and achieving a client satisfaction rating of 85%. An investment in new notebook computer technology will enable your sales team to exceed these goals.

High Cost of Current Equipment
The 50 sales team members on staff are currently assigned desktop computer equipment ranging in age from 3 to 5 years. This equipment provides one fourth (1/4th) the speed and storage of notebook systems available today. The computer support team reports an average of 7 desktop computer break downs a month. Sales team computer support costs average $9,500 per month.

Low Return of Current Equipment
Sales team members spend 80% of their time in the field with
clients across their sales territory, leaving PC equipment unused in
the office. As a result, sales are delayed or lost because sales quotes
and product information is not available when meeting with clients.
Client product and service issues cannot be resolved onsite. Clients
must wait for issue resolution once the sales executive returns to the
office. This results in lower client satisfaction.

A Solution That Adds Value
In a recent customer survey, 57% of your clients were not satisfied
with sale team response times. An internal sales review

determined that 22% of lost sales ($12 million) were due to
inaccurate pricing and proposal delays. The introduction of new
notebook computers will reverse these findings by providing your
sales team with immediate access to vital information whether in
the office or at the client location.

The Dell Latitude D410 notebook computer is an industry leader
at a reasonable price. This notebook is ideal for sales teams who
travel frequently but need high performance, wireless capability
and long battery life in a highly portable, light weight system. List
price per unit is $1,298. With the 50 unit volume discount, the per
unit cost will be $1,038 for a total investment of $51,900.

Recommendation
I strongly recommend that you make this investment in new
notebook computers for your sales team. You will increase sales
revenue and improve client satisfaction by having access to
all critical sales information while meeting with your clients,
delivering accurate and timely price quotes, product information
and issue resolution.

As you can see, this memo is a drastic contrast to the previous
memo. This less than one page memo grabs the reader's attention
and motivates him or her to take action. The reader is drawn into the
content of the memo because it offers a solution to his or her goals
and challenges. The memo provides information to support the

investment needs and potential value to the organization supporting a sound financial decision.

It will take some time to change your memo writing style. It took me months before the memo writing process felt second nature. I still catch a few bad memos that go out during the rush of a hectic day and pay the price when they do.

Mastery of memos that persuade is something that every top performer must do. With some practice, your memo writing skills will improve to the point where you can successfully persuade your clients to follow and take action on your recommendations.

My Top Book Recommendations
If you would like to research this topic in more detail, I highly recommend the following books.

- The Elements of Business Writing: A Guide to Writing Clear, Concise Letters, Memos, Reports, Proposals, and Other Business Documents, by Gary Blake, Robert W. Bly, ISBN-13: 978-0020080954

- Business Grammar, Style & Usage: The Most Used Desk Reference for Articulate and Polished Business Writing and Speaking by Executives Worldwide, by Alicia Abell, ISBN-13: 978-1587620263

- Effective Business Writing :(A Guide For Those who Write On the Job) 2nd Edition Revised And Updated, by Maryann V. Piotrowski, ISBN-13: 978-0062733818

What will you learn next?

In the next chapter we focus on how you can overcome gatekeeper barriers, catapulting your business and career.

11. Overcoming Gatekeeper Barriers

Like most professionals, you probably run into gatekeeper roadblocks on a daily basis. Sometimes it seems like every time you try to make contact with an executive or decision maker you are stopped right in your tracks. The difference between an average performer and a top performer is not that they break through the roadblocks better; they have learned how to appreciate the role of a gatekeeper and the best way to communicate with them. Let's explore how you can overcome gatekeeper barriers, catapulting your business and career.

In this chapter you will learn:
- [ ] 3 types of gatekeepers and how to work with each
- [ ] 3 key tips and techniques for reaching your target client
- [ ] 3 steps to getting a call back using a fax machine

Nightmare or Reality?

John is a Senior Sales Executive for a large software company who has a recurring nightmare. He arrives at work, picks up the phone and tries to contact ten new prospective clients. For each call he makes, he reaches a company receptionist who informs him that the person he is trying to contact will not speak to salesman. After three hours of rejection, John accomplishes nothing.

It's now time for his lunch appointment with Judy, an IT Systems Analyst. John has been schmoozing Judy for six months trying to convince her company to buy his products. This is the tenth lunch they've had and Judy still shows interest in his products. At the end of lunch John asks Judy if she would setup a meeting with her manager so he can pitch his new products. For the tenth time, she says, "No." Judy states that her manager does not meet with salesman, and has made her the primary contact. Judy ends the lunch with a hand shake, asking John to keep in touch. Another two hour lunch and nothing accomplished.

It is now 2pm. John is driving across town for a 3pm meeting with a current client who is ready to throw out his software. John's goal is to clinch a meeting with the CIO in order to understand what problems the company is facing with his product and what he can do to turn this around. John stops by to see the CIO's assistant, Mary. John asks Mary to setup a meeting for him. She tells John the CIO does not want to meet with him. John begs and pleads to no avail. John starts arguing loudly with the assistant that he must get a meeting. Mary calls security to have John removed. As the guard throws John out of the building, he wakes up from his nightmare in a cold sweat, with the feeling he needs to find another line of work.

Have you ever had one of those days? John's nightmare is a reality for many professionals. A "gatekeeper" is the general term we use for the people that try to block you from reaching decision makers. Let's take a more detailed look at these gatekeepers and how you can turn tough gatekeepers into your best allies.

Who Are Client Gatekeepers?

You will encounter three different types of client gatekeepers that will throw down roadblocks. Understanding who they are and what they do is vital for you to get meetings with your target client. Top performers understand gatekeepers can be a valuable asset instead of a roadblock. First, we will take a look at the three types of gatekeepers. In the following sections we will discuss top performer tips and techniques for working with these gatekeepers.

1. Front Desk

The front desk gatekeeper includes receptionists, phone operators, personnel manning the lobby desk and all others on the front line screening calls or visitors. Their job is to make sure callers and visitors get connected with the right person at the right time. They must follow strict written company policies and many informal personal policies. For example, some executives might want all calls and visitors routed through their assistants. Others might want special customers to have direct access. Some might want gatekeepers to route all salesman and vendors to lower levels and never have access to an executive.

The front desk gatekeeper has one of the most hectic and thankless jobs. They are the first to hear complaints from outsiders and the first to be blamed from internal company personnel when something goes wrong. From 8am to 5pm this gatekeeper is handling a steady stream of calls and visitors. Many of the encounters are from salesman trying to mislead them, mad customers venting their frustration and angry vendors who want answers. Would you want this job?

This is a tough job and deserves your respect and admiration. Due to the hectic nature of their day, you might find that gatekeepers are not pleasant when you introduce yourself. Stay cool and calm. Treat them like you would your grandmother. And always say thank you.

2. Executive Assistant

The executive assistant gatekeeper includes those individuals with titles like secretary, assistant, personal assistant, or executive assistant. This gatekeeper works very closely with your target client. He or she manages your target client's schedule, sets up meetings, screens phone calls, prepares meeting minutes, performs research, develops and proofs executive memos. The list goes on. Make no mistake; an executive assistant is the second most powerful person in the organization. They know critical information such as future strategies, which vendors are on the black list, and internal changes on the horizon. Basically, the executive assistant is an advisor and confidante to your target client.

I could write a book on executive assistant stories. I developed many long term friendships with executive assistants and they go on and on about how salesmen, consultants and other professionals treat them. They are usually treated like uneducated, low level peons. They are talked down to and given little respect. The stories are many, but the end result is the same. If gatekeepers close the door to your target client, you will be denied access.

Treat an executive assistant as you would your target client. He or she can be one of your biggest allies. If treated with the respect he or she deserves, he or she will help keep the doors wide open for you.

3. Middle Management

Middle Management gatekeepers include those individuals who have the responsibility to lead teams, but have limited decision making authority. They are usually the point person for outside professionals. These gatekeepers evaluate their offerings and make recommendations to executive leaders. Titles for these individuals may include: director, manager, project manager, analyst, supervisor or specialist. This gatekeeper will provide you with the best disguised roadblocks. They will protect their territory and executives at all costs. When asked about decision makers, they will tell you that "he or she" will be making all decisions.

When working with a middle management gatekeeper, keep in mind that he or she is leading a team, department or project and most likely upper management has instructed them to work with outside professionals and report back to an executive. These gatekeepers are usually very organized, detail oriented and take their responsibilities very seriously. Provide this gatekeeper with all the information they request, but also use some of the following techniques to get to your target client.

Your own experience will most likely confirm that this gatekeeper provides the biggest roadblocks and is the most time consuming to work through. Your goal is to avoid this gatekeeper as a first contact, if at all possible.

Getting Through to Your Target Client

You have thoroughly prepared. Your research has uncovered the appropriate target client and their assistant's name. You have an understanding of their business, goals and strategy. Your value proposition has been fine tuned to meet the target company industry and apparent needs. Now you are ready to make first contact.

You are most likely to make ninety percent of your initial contacts by phone. The front desk gatekeeper will be your first contact. When he or she answers the phone, you hear "XYZ Company, how may I help you?" Many training programs have taught you to ask for your target client contact by name. You would say, "I would like to speak with the CEO, Mr. Executive". For obvious reasons, you intend to bypass all gatekeepers, get to the right person immediately and eliminate wasted time. In reality, this method creates immediate roadblocks.

Asking for the target client directly will initiate a slew of questions aimed to redirect you to someone else. For example, you might hear questions like: "Who is calling?", "What is your reason for calling?", "What are you trying to sell?", or "Are you a vendor?" I'm sure you have heard these and many more during your career. When you initiate this questioning process, no matter what your answers, the end response by the front desk gatekeeper will be "Mr. Jones does not directly handle this, let me transfer you to Mr. Middle-Management. He will be happy to help you with this." There you go. You have now stepped on the carousel, going around and around, ending up at the same place you started.

Let's review the top three tips and techniques that top performers use.

1. Call the Executive Assistant

To improve your first contact success rate in the shortest timeframe possible, your first contact should be to the executive assistant. Why? Remember, the executive assistant is the second most influential contact.. Additionally, he or she is one of the most accessible influencers. Avoid front desk and middle management gatekeepers if at all possible. If you are able to obtain the direct phone number for the executive assistant during your initial research, then use it. Call the executive assistant directly. We will discuss this more later. If you make your first call and other gatekeepers answer, here is what you do. In a polite confident voice, respond, "Please connect me with Andy Assistant. Thank you." Believe it or not, every time I have used this response, I am put through to the assistant immediately, no questions asked.

Let's take a quick look at the statement again and break it down:
- "Please" – This is a very polite way to start. Gatekeepers will be more open to your request. Please is a word that gatekeepers rarely hear, therefore, they appreciate it.
- "Connect me with Andy Assistant" – This is a simple and straight forward request for action.
- "Thank you." – This is a very polite way to end a request. It is also another rarely heard phrase that the gatekeeper will remember. You need to make it a habit to end with a "thank you" anytime you request or receive information.

Within seconds the gatekeeper will connect you to the executive assistant.

2. Tell the Truth, the Whole Truth

Never mislead or lie to a gatekeeper, no matter what. Many professionals have been trained to stretch the truth or do anything to get a meeting with a target client. For example, they might say, "Hello, this is Dave, a good friend of Mr. Executive. He is waiting for my call. Please put me through to him". No matter the situation, or what questions the gatekeeper asks, always tell the truth. When you appear to be a liar, people perceive you as slimy, unprofessional, unethical. Target clients are not interested in doing business with dishonest people. . As the old saying goes, "Honesty is the best policy." Top performers live by this saying.

Let's look at a few examples of what you should avoid.
- Telling the gatekeeper you know the target client, when you do not.
- Telling the gatekeeper you have an appointment, when you do not.
- Telling the gatekeeper you were told to call the target client back, when you were not.
- Threatening the gatekeeper he or she will be fired if he or she doesn't connect you.

3. Handling an Interrogation

If you have follow the ideas and techniques mentioned above, you will most likely be talking with your target client and not need this section. Unfortunately, there are occasions when you will run into a gatekeeper that is power hungry and confrontational. He or she will do anything to keep you away from the target client. To be successful in getting through, you must remain calm, confident and bring some humor to the conversation.

When being hit with question after question, you should follow these rules:
DO:
- Keep your voice calm
- Keep answers at a high level
- Maintain focus on their organization goals and challenges

- Focus your responses on solution benefits and value

DON'T:
- Argue with the gatekeeper
- Use a confrontational tone of voice
- Use the name of your product or service
- Use technical jargon or acronyms

Here is an example of how a top performer would answer one of those endless interrogation questions.

Gatekeeper: "What are you really calling about?"

You: "I am going to provide Mr. Executive the opportunity to discuss how other Financial Services organizations have reduced IT costs by 32%."

Stay confident, keep you cool and stay focused on your value.

My Top Book Recommendations
If you would like to research this topic in more detail, I highly recommend the following books.

- Barry Farber's Guide To Handling Sales Objections, by Barry J. Farber, ISBN-13: 978-1564147738

- Little Red Book of Selling: 12.5 Principles of Sales Greatness, by Jeffrey Gitomer, ISBN-13: 978-1885167606

- Never Eat Alone: And Other Secrets to Success, One Relationship at a Time, by Keith Ferrazzi, Tahl Raz, ISBN-13: 978-0385512053

What will you learn next?

In the next chapter we focus on how you can promote yourself to the top of your profession, resulting in clients begging you to take the assignment.

12. Promote Yourself to The Top of Your Profession

Are you cold calling clients instead of them calling you? Are you looking to advance quickly through the top ranks of your organization with little success? Are you hunting for that next opportunity and have no offers? You could be the most brilliant, experienced individual in your profession, but if clients don't know about the value you deliver, they will most likely never seek you and select you for an assignment. We will now discover how top performers promote themselves to the top of their profession, resulting in clients begging them to take the assignment.

In this chapter you will learn:
- ☐ 10 best self promotion techniques that top performers use
- ☐ 12 additional business resources to use in self promotion
- ☐ 50+ tips and techniques to use when executing a self promotion plan

Following the Best Path

Neal is a senior manager for a major management consulting firm. Within the firm he is the "go to" guy. His creative thinking and high business intelligence are major assets to the company. Unfortunately, throughout most of his career, he was the "brilliant unknown guru". He can solve the most difficult business problems but is terrible at promoting his own abilities and skills.

Neal's goal from the beginning of his career was to become a firm partner using his impressive consulting abilities. Year after year management passed him over for promotion. At one of his annual reviews, his managing partner finally told Neal that he would never make partner. This was because even though Neal was a brilliant consultant, he lacked good communication skills. Deficient communication skills limited his ability to bring in new clients or retain additional services from current clients. The lack of generating revenue limited his pay and killed any chance for promotion.

Being "the guru" in your professional isn't everything. As Neal's example illustrates, you must be able to communicate with others if you want to maximize career advancement, earn the highest wages or become a top performer.

Mike, on the other hand, a partner for a major management consulting firm, took a different path. Mike was a good management consultant. His work was sound and delivered value to his customers. He differentiated himself from everyone else by mastering his communication skills. Going a step further, he used these skills to promote his consulting capabilities internally and externally.

Mike's communication and self promotion resulted in:
- work products and proposals that were clear, concise and loved by clients;
- clients opening up to him two minutes after meeting him;
- clients seeking him personally;

- clients signing $10 million contracts again and again;
- referrals by current clients that became the norm.

Mike was promoted to partner in a record breaking six years instead of the normal ten years for other partners. Mike is a highly paid, highly respected and a highly sought after management consultant. He is at the top of his game at a very young age.

What did Mike do differently? First, Mike understood the importance of communication skills. From the beginning of his career he spent his spare time perfecting his communication skills just like I describe in this book. Second, he also understood the importance of self promotion. At every opportunity he would promote his capabilities and performance.

Do you dream of being a top performer? The powerful tools I provide in this book will help you develop the skills you need to become a top performer. Your goal of being a top performer is within your grasp if you promote yourself. How much you promote yourself will depend on how far and how fast you want to go.

Top 10 Self Promotion Tips

In this chapter, I'm going to give you the ten best self promotion techniques that top performers use.

1. Create a Personal Website

A website is essential for promoting yourself to the world. Where else can you get exposure to millions of people at little cost? Websites are not just for large companies or independent consultants. Anyone who wants to promote his or her ideas and expertise can benefit. Your views and ideas will be just one click away. The best part is, you can update your information whenever you like and it will be available within minutes. Share your website address with everyone you encounter. You never know who will be in need of your expertise. Include the site address on your business card, email signature and any written correspondence.

Let's take a look at what you should include on your website:

- **Bio**. Provide a short biography covering your accomplishments, certifications, areas of specialty, education and interests. This should be no more than a one page overview of who you are.

- **Area of Specialty**. Provide a page covering your area of expertise. Describe the depth of your knowledge and what you can offer your future clients, friends or readers of your site. Describe your accomplishments and how others have gained value from your capabilities.

- **Appearances**. Do you speak at conferences, seminars or local events? Do you attend local industry or organization meetings? If you do, list them on you site. Include the date, time, location, organization and if you are speaking, the topic title. You want to show your wide range of interests and locations where people can come to meet you, the expert.

- **Articles**. Have you written any articles? Whether they are published or not, put all your articles on the website. Everyone is interested in new ideas or better ways of doing things. With this exposure, major newspapers, magazines or newsletters might pick them up.

- **References**. References include quotes and testimonials from clients, peers, managers or anyone else who has found your expertise valuable. By providing these quotes, you build credibility with potential clients who are looking for someone in your specialty. For example, a quote may look like this: "James delivered a human resources software assessment that exceeded our expectations and saved us $50,000 (Ken Collins – CIO, XYZ Company)" Make sure you have approvals to use the quote. Always include the person's name, title and company.

- **Top 10 Lists**: Everyone loves to read top 10 lists. You can provide a top 10 "How To" list within your specialty area. You could also include top 10 lists for many other areas like, "My Top 10 Favorite Business Books" or "My Top 10 Favorite Vacation Spots". You get the picture. Create a top 10 list for anything that interests you and might be beneficial for anyone looking at your site.

- **Contact Me**. List an e-mail address where clients can reach you. You could also include your phone number if you prefer.

2. Speak Anywhere and Everywhere

Get out there and show off your knowledge and experience. Speaking in front of a client provides many benefits. Clients see you as an expert because you are in the front of the room speaking. You have the undivided attention of the client and can influence his or her thoughts and future actions. One speaking engagement can lead to many more. Future clients can be in the audience and will look to put you at the top of their list for new work assignments.

Speak in front of anyone who will listen. Some speaking engagements are paid, but most are not. Don't worry about payment. The exposure provides the greatest value. No speaking engagement is too small.

Here are a few examples on where you can start speaking:
- Company meetings and events
- Company Lunch-N-Learn meetings
- Charity events
- Boy Scouts or other club events
- PTA Meetings
- Industry Association meetings
- Conferences

- Seminars
- Toastmaster Events
- Religious Groups
- Job Search and Networking Groups
- User Groups
- Chamber of Commerce meetings

3. Write Articles

Everyone respects the written word. This translates into readers considering the author an authority on the subject, the "go to" person for additional information. By writing a one or two page article, you can quickly help readers solve problems, motivate them to achieve more or introduce new ideas.

You think this is too difficult? Are you sure? Have you written down your thoughts since elementary school or kept a diary or journal at one time or another? Writing an article is just as easy. First, pick a topic where you have experience, for example, the topic "How to Prepare for an Interview". Next, create an outline with the major points you want to cover. This includes an introduction, three to five major points you want to address and then the summary or conclusion. Last, following your outline, start writing down the information you want to present in the article. When you're finished, take a break and then go back to review, edit and revise the article to make sure the information flows and is easily readable. It's easy to overlook you own mistakes. Have someone else look over your work. There you are! Within a couple hours you are now an author and expert in your field.

Next, you need to distribute your article so people can see why you are an expert and someone who should be sought out to solve their problems. You can submit your articles to a variety of forums including:

- Company websites
- Company newsletters
- Your website

- Newspapers
- Magazines
- Industry newsletters
- Online discussion groups like in Yahoo
- Online article directories
- Websites related to the topic
- Online article distribution sites, www.submityourarticle. com or www.websubmitarticles.com

4. Write a Book

After experiencing the success from publishing a few articles, you might consider taking the next step- publishing a book. Think about all the top performers that you admire. I bet they have published at least one book. It's more likely they have many. Top performers understand that publishing a book is key to their success. A published book gives you tremendous credibility as the authority on the subject.

Have you ever been discussing a subject and during the discussion said, "He wrote a book on this?" You automatically gave the author the status of the most knowledgeable expert on the topic. If you needed more information on the subject, who would you contact? Yes, the author of the book. Your book will draw a huge awareness to your talents and expertise. This awareness, credibility and top performer status will translate into career success, new business, increased income or many more benefits.

Do you have enough information for a book? The average business book is 200 pages or 80,000 words. This is equivalent to about 134 pages typed in 12 pt single spaced format. What should you do if you only have enough information to fill a 24 page book or even just a 10 page book? Why not create a booklet? Many times this is just as effective as a 200 page business book. Booklets are very successful since they usually address a specific topic and are a quick read.

Here are the steps to follow when publishing your first book:
- Come up with a subject that is new or a twist on previous published work.
- Research other books, articles and websites on the topic.
- Identify your target audience and the reader issues you are trying to solve.
- Outline your topic into no more than 20 chapters with 10 to 15 major points per chapter.
- Perform interviews, obtain quotes and statistics supporting your material.
- Write your book.
- Edit your book.
- Create an agent/publisher sales letter promoting your book.
- Offer book to agents, publishers or self publish.

Here are a few helpful resources:
- Steve Manning, "How To Write A Book On Anything In 14 Days or Less" www.writeabooknow.com
- Tom & Marilyn Ross, "The Complete Guide To Self-Publishing" www.about-books.com

5. Publish a Newsletter

Many professionals underestimate the huge value of a newsletter. Newsletters connect you with your internal and external clients on a continuous basis. You provide them with new information while subtly selling them on your products and services.

Depending on your profession and objectives, there are many types of newsletters that will make you successful. The key is to determine your target audience.. Here are a few ideas to help you get started. Write a newsletter that will focus on a specific:
- industry;
- profession;
- career role;
- project
- company;
- department.

There are two types of newsletters you could create. First is the "printed newsletter". This is a hardcopy newsletter that you send through the mail and distribute at events. Your newsletter can be full color or black and white. Both work well, but a full color newsletter is attractive if you have the budget.

Second is the "e-newsletter". An electronic newsletter is the simplest and least expensive to produce. You can produce each issue in a text or html format and send it to your subscribers via e-mail. You should also make the e-newsletter available on your website. Getting subscribers is very easy. You can obtain their email addresses from events, your website, previous newsletters forwarded to others and your own personal client list.

No matter what format you use, your newsletter must contain information that the subscribers will find valuable. Omit sales and marketing information. If you are only advertising your products and services, you will quickly you're your subscriber base. Provide "value", which could include ways to increase sales, reduce costs, improve personal performance, increase productivity or make the subscriber's life easier. You get the idea.

Great newsletter content is crucial to a successful newsletter. Of course, you will have your company name, your contact information and relevant links to your website in the newsletter. Most importantly you will have one or more articles relevant to your subscribers' interests.

When producing your newsletter, whether electronic or printed, you should provide the following information:

At the Top
- Newsletter name
- Your Name, email, phone number, address and website link.
- Issue date

Middle
- In This Issue (a list or index of the articles or subject matter titles)
- Article or Article Short Description (if this is an electronic newsletter, provide a paragraph description of the article and then provide a link to the full article on your website)

End
- Links to related websites or information
- Request feedback or surveys
- Provide special offers

There are many different newsletter layout and format types available today. Do a web search and investigate the different styles and capabilities. Pick one that best matches your target audience preferences.

Overall, you can measure the value of your newsletter by future income and career/professional advancement. Subscribers will come to trust you, your viewpoints and straight forward facts. Your credibility will dramatically increase over time.

6. Create a Blog

What is a blog? A blog, short for "web log", is one of the latest innovations hitting the internet like storm. Basically, a blog is a web- based journal that is updated frequently and is intended to be viewed by any interested party on the web. It is intended to be a communication tool where you can write down thoughts, opinions, or questions and interact with others. Writing a personal blog can be very entertaining and business blogs can be a very powerful tool allowing you to communicate with potential customers. Best of all, blogs can help you generate new sales channels in a very cost effective manner.

You can use your blog to talk about current projects, new products and services, innovative ideas, your speaking appearances or just about anything. You should keep your blog focused around a specific topic area. This will help you attract and retain others with the same interests and needs. Focus on your specialty area, industry or profession.

How big is blogging? According to the blog tracking firm Technorati at www.technorati.com, there are currently 48.3 million sites with blogs being tracked and 80,000 more added every day. More importantly, over 30% of internet users are reading blogs. That can translate into a significant amount of potential clients!

To make the most of your blog, keep it active and updated, giving readers a reason to return to your site. Make your blog as interactive as possible. Allow readers to ask questions and post comments. Encourage traffic to your blog site by including keywords in your titles.

Are you ready to get started? Read blogs that teach you how to blog. Here are a few that I recommend.
- ProBlogger, www.problogger.net- This is a great resource on how to become a blogger.
- BlogWrite for CEO's, www.blogwriteforceos.com- This provides blogging information focused at the executive level.
- The Blog Herald, www.blogherald.com – This provides general information on blogging and blog news.
- Blog Top Sites, www.blogtopsites.com- This helps you search the top blog sites by category.

There are many other blogs that will provide you with valuable information. Do a Google search for blogs and any specific topic you like. See what is out there.

You can start off with a personal blog or go directly to a business blog. Test a few blog systems and see if they meet your needs and objectives.

I suggest you check out these blog systems:
- Blogger, www.blogger.com – This is a free blogging system with limited capabilities.
- Typepad, www.sixapart.com/typepad- This offers great capabilities with a minimal monthly fee.
- BlogHarbor, www.blogharber.com –This offers very good capabilities with a minimal monthly fee

7. Send Press Releases

Are you looking for free advertising about you or your business? Look no further than the power of a press release. Imagine the exposure you will get when you have a great story to tell and it is distributed through hundreds of media and news feeds.

Have you completed a successful project? Are you hosting a seminar? Are you offering a new product or service? These and many other topics are just what the media seeks. Once you submit your press release, it may very well appear in newspapers, magazines, online directories, and websites. The press release may also attract the attention of TV and radio outlets. I have seen many of these initial press releases turn into TV and radio interviews. If your goal is to get your name and successes out into the public eye whether locally, nationally or globally, then press releases are a wonderful tool for meeting your goals.

When should you submit a press release? Let's take a look at a sample list of very effective topics that will grab the attention of the media and readers.

Submit a press release about:
- a business association or club you're starting;
- a celebrity who is endorsing your business;
- a charity event you're sponsoring;
- a free newsletter you're publishing;
- a joint venture with another business;
- a new book you published;
- a seminar workshop or training class you're hosting;

- a successful project you have completed;
- a trade show you're sponsoring;
- an award that you or your business has won;
- free seminars you're holding or leading;
- the new products or services you're offering;
- the results of a research survey you have completed;
- your new web site.

When preparing your press release, take into account the following advice from top performers:

- Place the date and your contact information at the top of the press release.
- Proofread and edit your press release.
- Send your press release to media related to the topic of your press release.
- Your first paragraph should keep the reader's attention and entice them to read further.
- Your press release body should be centered on a story and how you deliver benefits and value.
- Your press release should be news, not a marketing statement.
- Your press release should be one page or less.
- Your press release title should grab the reader's attention.

You have many different options when submitting a press release for distribution. Here are few directions you can take.

- Submit press releases directly to the media targets via e-mail or fax. Research how each media outlet accepts press releases and any restrictions that might apply.
- Submit press releases online through mass distribution sites. For a fee, these sites will push out your press release to many media types (websites, news feeds and traditional media.). I recommend taking a look at the following sites.
  - o PRWeb, www.prweb.com
  - o PR Newswire, www.prnewswire.com
  - o 24-7 Press Release, www.24-7pressrelease.com

8. Accomplishments List

Keep a list of everything you accomplish. This list will become invaluable when you are talking with your boss, clients, partners, or the media. You might remember everything you have done in the past six months, but most people can't remember what they accomplished 18 months ago. Not many professionals can whip out all their accomplishments when put on the spot. How good will you look when a new clients asks you, "What type of grocery retail experience do you have?" You can confidently and quickly rattle off ten examples including the initial challenges, your solution and the value they achieved. Or, what about when the president of an industry organization would like to know what qualifications you have for speaking at an international conference? Once again, within seconds you can provide a list of related seminars, workshops and presentations you have hosted. Think of all the possible situations where this will make you stand out as the top performer in your profession.

You can create your accomplishments list using many different formats. Your list can be hand written in a journal, stored in a database or spreadsheet or entered into a software application. Use the format that is most comfortable for you. I personally use an Excel Spreadsheet. I find this easy to enter and organize my information. It is also very easy to sort and filter information.

Let's take a look at what you could include in your accomplishment list:
- Successful projects
- Product and services delivered
- Articles published
- Speaking engagements at seminars and conferences
- Books published
- Patents received
- Certifications
- Industry groups and association membership
- Volunteer work

9. Network for Referrals

You find seventy percent of new job offers and new clients through your network of acquaintances. These come directly from your contact or through referrals from those contacts. The secret to building a great network is to concentrate on the quality of the relationships you build, not the quantity of contacts. The best way to think about building a network is to think you are building business alliances. In this way, you help each other become more successful.

With all the demands on your time made by your business, professional and personal lives, it is tempting to assign a lower priority to networking. This can be a mistake. You need to keep networking at the top of your "to do" list and find the time to participate. Make it a priority.

Let's take a look at the places where you can start building a network:
- Industry events
- Conferences and seminars
- Business events (Chamber of Commerce meetings, Kiwanis, etc.)
- Universities and training classes
- Organized networking events
- Current client
- Friends and family
- Religious organizations and events

Are you ready to get started? Here are a few ideas to improve your networking experience:
- Create a networking plan (where, when, who to target).
- Prepare how you will introduce yourself and describe what you do.
- Get involved with industry organizations.
- Practice good communication skills described in this book.
- Participate - Act like you are the host of the event.

- Work on building a long term relationship.
- Don't beat around the bush; ask for what you want.
- Organize your network of names in a journal, spreadsheet, or Outlook, ACT!
- Relax and have a great time.

Whenever you get a referral from one of your contacts, verify that the person knows you will be calling. Then, call the person as soon as possible.

A good way to introduce yourself would be, "Hello Mr. Smith. This is Jim Johnson. Jennifer Jones, your VP of Sales, asked me to call you and I promised her I would."

10. Teach a Class

You can quickly establish yourself as an expert in your field by teaching classes. Think of all the instructors you have had in your life time. When you had a question, you went to the instructor covering that topic. When your peers asked a question about this topic, you gave them the name and number for the instructor who taught the class. Teaching a class is a great way to promote yourself as an expert in your field.

What should you teach? There are two criteria that you must meet to be successful. First, you need to teach a topic that is in critical need by your target audience or client base. Talk with as many people as you can to find topics of interest to them. Discuss how they will take advantage of this information. How will they benefit? For example, will it increase their productivity 20% or increase sales by 30%? Once you have done this analysis, determine which class would provide the most benefit for your target audience.

Second, you need to have knowledge and experience with this topic area. It is hard to convince a class that you are an expert when you have no practical experience with the topic. If you were a Chief Information Officer attending a class on reducing technology costs, would you feel you got your money's worth if the instructor was an insurance sales specialist with limited technology experience? Would you call this person a week later for a consultation? I don't think so. Stick with topics that are within your focus area where you have practical knowledge and experience you can share with others.

Don't worry about what they will pay you. What matters is you're getting out there in front of your current and future clients sharing your deep knowledge and expertise. You are showcasing your abilities and demonstrating why you are at the top of your profession.

You can find teaching opportunities at:
- industry group conferences and chapter meetings;
- within your own company;
- universities;
- adult education programs;
- recreation centers;
- chamber of commerce meetings.

Your Next Step
Establishing yourself as the top professional in your field takes time, planning and dedication. Start now by implementing a couple of items from the above top 10 list, or take a shot at all ten. Soon people will be seeking you out. From there, it's up to you on how big and how far you want to take your career or business.

Your options as a top performer will be unlimited.

My Top Book Recommendations
If you would like to research this topic in more detail, I highly recommend the following books.

- Value Forward Marketing: How to Use Thought Leadership and Return-on-Investment Calculations to

Cost Effectively Turn Prospects Into Buyers by Paul R. Dimodica, ISBN-13: 978-1933598352

- 49 Marketing Secrets (That Work) to Grow Sales by Ronald Finklestein, Dennis Sommer (Contributor) ISBN-13: 978-1600372483

- The New Rules of Marketing and PR: How to Use News Releases, Blogs, Podcasting, Viral Marketing and Online Media to Reach Buyers Directly by David Meerman Scott, ISBN-13: 978-0470113455

- Guerrilla Marketing, 4th edition: Easy and Inexpensive Strategies for Making Big Profits from Your Small Business by Jay Conrad Levinson, ISBN-13: 978-0618785919

What will you learn next?

In the next chapter we focus on how you can become a household name and eliminate the need for marketing.

13. Be Your Client's First Call - Become a Household Name

How would you like to run a successful business that didn't need marketing? You have customers calling you 24 hours a day nonstop, more business than you can handle and no need for a marketing budget. This is what can happen when you become a "Household Name". A "Household Name" is that person or business that everyone thinks of when they have a serious problem that must be fixed. They are the expert, specialist, or guru that immediately comes to mind.

In this chapter you will learn:
- [ ] 4 characteristics needed to become a Household Name
- [ ] Actions items you can start implementing today
- [ ] Why this strategy is critical to your business growth

If you are in need of investment help, does the name Charles Schwab and Peter Block come to mind? Do you think of Tom Peters and Stephen Covey when you are having management issues? If you are having real-estate development issues, does the name Donald Trump come to mind? When you are faced with sales and leadership challenges, do you immediately start contracting Dennis Sommer at 800-627-6512 or www.dennissommer.com ? If not, you should. That's me. You get my point. Do you think any of these business professionals really need to market their businesses. I don't think so. How different would your business be if your name first comes to mind when your customer needs help? When you think about it, becoming a "Household Name" should be your highest business priority.

Let's take a look at how you can become a "Household Name" in your market and industry.

Every successful business person had to start somewhere. Most likely they were in the same position you're in today. Start by implementing one marketing idea, then another. Monitor your success and adjust your strategy accordingly. As the advice from this book increases your market share and name recognition, you must also focus on your second step toward "Household Name" status.

Your second step involves developing the characteristics of a "Household Name". These characteristics are what makes a person or business a Household Name vs. just someone that is in business. These characteristics make you stand out above everyone else. In your customer's mind, you will be the only one that can help them solve his or her problem. When these characteristics become second nature to you and your organization, you will be well on your way to success beyond your dreams.

Let's take a look at the key characteristics of a "Household Name" broken out by Customer Service, Communication, Knowledge and Building Strong Relationships.

Superior Customer Service

I recently received a call from the CEO of a highly successful start-up firm. Jerry, the CEO, was very concerned about reports showing customer satisfaction was at an all time low. During the initial launch of the firm, Jerry expected to have a few bumps in the road. Two years after the initial launch, the company's customer satisfaction numbers were still low and declining.

After reviewing the performance measurements, expectations and the impact this challenge was taking on the firm, we decided to perform a complete Customer Service Assessment covering the sales, finance, services and management teams. Our objective was to pinpoint specific areas where we could improve customer service and make recommendations on how we could implement these improvements. Jerry wanted his company to become a "Household Name".

Here is what we found. The firm's ability to deliver a superior service and their knowledge of the industry was beyond reproach. These were the two factors that made them successful. The root cause of their customer satisfaction challenges was from their customer service philosophy. Their focus on customer service started once a client complained. At that point they were committed to resolving the issue and did everything to keep the client as a customer.

The solution to this challenge was focusing on customer service even before a client became a client. By focusing on customer service from the first initial client meeting, the firm could eliminate customer complaints instead of reacting to them once they occurred. Even though it is too soon to measure the impact of our training and mentoring solution, customer complaints from new clients have been declining drastically.

1. Focus on The Customer
A "Household Name" always provides superior customer service. Household Names focus on the customer instead of themselves and

their business. The focus on great customer service turns satisfied customers into lifelong loyal customers.

2. Positive Attitude

A positive attitude, focused attention, and commitment to resolving customer complaints will have a huge impact on customer satisfaction and the likelihood your customer will buy from you again and again.

3. Offer a Guarantee

Guarantee your offering and stand by it. Offer an unconditional money back guarantee on all products and services.

4. Focus on the Customer's Goal

Help customers achieve their goals, not yours. Your goals will be exceeded when you help customers solve their problems.

5. Recommend Other Solutions

Have the best interest of the customer in mind. Try to bring a customer with a problem together with an offering that helps them solve it. If you don't have the exact solution they require, recommend other business solutions that could help them.

6. It's Okay to Disagree

Customers are not "always" right. Disagree with a customer, in a polite professional manner, in order to help them make a better decision.

Strong Communication

Take a moment and think about a "Household Name" in your industry. Do they rattle off statistics, techno jargon, and other mumbo jumbo that could only be understood by a NASA scientist? Do they go on forever lecturing you on incomprehensible topics and you never have a chance to talk? Most likely your answer is, "No".

A "Household Name" has the ability to sit down and listen to clients. Then, a "Household Name" translates a very complex solution into terms that a six year old can understand. They keep it simple.

A "Household Name" focuses on improving written, verbal, and listening skills. When dealing with customers you must become the master communicator.

1. Communicate Your Value
Always tell your customer why they should buy/use your solution. Use plain English (no technical terminology) and describe the benefits. Example: "Produce a widget in ½ the time" or "Services are performed in ½ the time and at ½ the cost".

2. Listen Naively
Listen naively instead of defending and debating. Keeping an open, unbiased mind and the customer talking, provides valuable information that you can address in the future.

3. Tell a Story
Customers will better understand information if told as a story. Instead of showing numbers, statistics and technical points, tell them a story about customer experiences with the offering, how they used it, and the value they received.

4. Use Simple Language
You have a 50% greater chance of success by translating raw data into simple words, knowledge, and wisdom that customers can use to make smart decisions. Turn raw data into a story.

5. Demonstrate Your Solution
Highlight and demonstrate how easy your solution is to use.

Tremendous Knowledge

One of my favorite conversations to have with salesmen, consultants, business owners and so called experts when I am on the road is this: "Tell me about the solutions you provide and how they compare to your competition". I find this to be the most enlightening question to determine how knowledgeable this professional is in their industry. My unofficial findings might surprise you. Only 50% of them carry on a fulfilling conversation about their own solutions. Even more depressing is that only 10% of these professionals can describe the pros and cons comparing their solution to their primary competitor. My favorite response is, "I just sell what I'm told too. I don't need to understand the product or my competitors' products."

Would you hire a professional or purchase a solution from someone who didn't take the time to learn about his or her industry or products? Would you have confidence in his or her solution? I didn't think so. So what impression do you leave with your customers?

"Household Names" not only become the expert in their own solutions, they also become an expert on their competitors and the customer's industry.

1. Allocate Your Time
Spend 60% of your time with customers, 20% learning more about your offering and trade craft, and 20% on other business needs like management and administration.

2. Know Thy Competitor
No one should know more about your offering and your competitor's offerings than you. Build confidence by knowing both the technical specifications and their applications.

3. Know Thy Industry
Learn more about your industry. The more you read and learn, the greater your likelihood to be among the first to identify meaningful solutions.

4. Talk about Your Competition
Learn to talk more about your competition, what the customers like, and what they dislike.

Builds Strong Relationships

A big portion of my work with clients focuses on improving sales by improving their relationship with the customer. In this fast paced world, many professionals and organizations are so focused on short term goals; they have forgotten one of the most important success factors. People buy relationships not products. It's hard to focus on the customer when you are dealing with monthly quota goals, internal politics, investors, organizational changes, and the overflow of email and voice-mail requests requiring immediate responses. Unfortunately, if you ignore your customer, they won't be a customer for long.

Robert, the President of a small technology company and long time client came to me with a challenge. His goal was to improve customer retention by 30% while improving sales margins by 25%. The organization as a whole was so busy growing and focusing on short term issues, they forgot how they became successful. They were so focused on internal issues, they forgot about the customer. We called this project "Getting Back to Basics".

To improve customer retention, we worked on developing relationships with their customers instead of just taking orders. The customer became top priority for every employee. Everything else was a lower priority. Second, we revamped the selling and billing processes to make it easier for the customer to do business with them. This improved customer satisfaction and reduced the sales cycle by 50%. These changes have dramatically improved their business and have turned average customers into loyal customers. Within 18 months, customer retention improved 37% while sales margins improved 26%. In the end, building strong customer relationships and getting back to the basics, has exceeded everyone's expectations.

Connecting with customers on a personal and professional level will build a strong customer relationship turning them into lifetime loyal customers.

1. Reduce Customer Stress

The easier it is for customers to do business with you, the greater their likelihood of repurchasing. For example, make the selling process as easy as possible. A long, complex selling process will turn off customers and drive them to your competitors.

2. Pay Attention To Detail

Customers make a direct connection between attention to detail and competence. Pay attention to such details as spelling, what you say, out of place items, grooming or dress.

3. Do A Road Show

Do a 20 customer road show twice a year. Nothing beats going into the field and meeting customers face- to- face to better understand what they need and show them what you have to offer.

4. Over Deliver

Create a pattern of dependability by making small promises and over delivering on results.

5. Be Honest

Be an honest adviser. Present both the strengths and weaknesses of your offering. It is better for the customer to learn about your weaknesses now than to discover them later.

6. Stay Upbeat

Keep your tone upbeat. Make a point to elevate the moods of people around you. Hearing your name should lift their mood.

7. Be Likeable

Customers prefer to buy from people they like. Being likeable is as simple as helping customers feel happy, relaxed, and even feel good about themselves.

Are you ready to go beyond marketing and become a "Household Name"?

Are you prepared to become a leader in your industry?

Starting today, take the next steps to make it happen.

My Top Book Recommendations
If you would like to research this topic in more detail, I highly recommend the following books.

- Sales Management Power Strategies: Building a replicable and scalable sales process by Paul R. Dimodica, ISBN-13: 978-1933598284

- Value Forward Selling: How to sell to management by Paul R. Dimodica, ISBN-13: 978-1933598314

- Good to Great: Why Some Companies Make the Leap... and Others Don't by Jim Collins ISBN-13: 978-0066620992

Conclusion - Where Do You Go From Here?

Congratulations! You've just completed this book and are now at the beginning of your journey to become a top performer in your profession.

As your new journey begins, I would like to leave you with a few pieces of advice that will help you jump start the use of the material you just read.

1. Take the proven techniques from this book and make them your own. Adjust them to match your own professional style.

2. Start using the approaches and techniques tomorrow. Don't wait. You might hesitate or feel awkward at first, however the more you put them to use, the better your results.

3. Keep your eye on the end goal. If you want to become a top performer you will need focus, determination and passion. Think about your goal as soon as you wake up and right before going to sleep at night.

May all your dreams come true!

Think big, take action and enjoy your success!

My Book Recommendations

If you would like to research this topic in more detail, I highly recommend the following books.

Success Models – How to become a leader in your profession
- The 4-Hour Workweek: Escape 9-5, Live Anywhere, and Join the New Rich, by Timothy Ferriss, ISBN-13: 978-0307353139
- Getting Things Done: The Art of Stress-Free Productivity, by David Allen, ISBN-13: 978-0142000281
- The Tipping Point: How Little Things Can Make a Big Difference, by Malcolm Gladwell, ISBN-13: 978-0316346627

Questioning–How to ask powerful, smart and insightful questions
- Leading with Questions: How Leaders Find the Right Solutions By Knowing What To Ask, by Michael J. Marquardt, ISBN-13: 978-0787977467
- How to Ask Great Questions: Guide Your Group to Discovery With These Proven Techniques, by Karen Lee-Thorp, ISBN-13: 978-1576830789
- Questions That Work: How to Ask Questions That Will Help You Succeed in Any Business Situation, by Andrew Finlayson, ISBN-13: 978-0814473290

Listening – How to become and effective listener
- Listening: The Forgotten Skill: A Self-Teaching Guide, by Madelyn Burley-Allen, ISBN-13: 978-0471015871
- Are You Really Listening?: Keys to Successful Communication, by Paul J., Ph.D. Donoghue, Mary E. Siegel, ISBN-13: 978-1893732889
- Listen Up!: How to Communicate Effectively at Work, by Eunice Lemay, Jane Schwamberger, ISBN-13: 978-0978805852

Objection Handling – How to eliminate client objections and resistance
- Selling 101: What Every Successful Sales Professional Needs to Know, by Zig Ziglar, ISBN-13: 978-0785264811
- How to Win Friends & Influence People, by Dale Carnegie, ISBN-13: 978-0671027032
- How to Close Every Sale, by Joe Girard, ISBN-13: 978-0446389297

Preparing a Presentation – How to inspire and motivate and audience
- Clear and to the Point: 8 Psychological Principles for Compelling PowerPoint Presentations, by Stephen M. Kosslyn, ISBN-13: 978-0195320695
- Presenting to Win: The Art of Telling Your Story, by Jerry Weissman, ISBN-13: 978-0130464132
- The Exceptional Presenter: A Proven Formula to Open Up and Own the Room, by Timothy J. Koegel, ISBN-13: 978-1929774449

Delivering a Presentation – How to persuade your client to your recommendations
- Public Speaking (8th Edition), by Michael Osborn, Suzanne Osborn, Randall Osborn, ISBN-13: 978-0205584567

- Public Speaking: An Audience-Centered Approach (6th Edition), by Steven A. Beebe, Susan J. Beebe, ISBN-13: 978-0205449835
- There's No Such Thing as Public Speaking: Make Any Presentation or Speech as Persuasive as a One-on-One Conversation, by Jeanette and Roy Henderson, ISBN-13: 978-0735204157

Planning a Meeting – How to plan the most effective meeting

- The Complete Idiot's Guide to Meeting & Event Planning, 2nd Edition, by Robin E. Craven, Lynn Johnson Golabowski, ISBN-13: 978-1592574629
- Successful Meetings: How to Plan, Prepare, and Execute Top-Notch Business Meetings, by Shri Henkel, ISBN-13: 978-0910627917
- Plan and Conduct Effective Meetings: 24 Steps to Generate Meaningful Results, by Barbara J Streibel, ISBN-13: 978-0071498319

Facilitating a Meeting – How to run the most effective meeting

- Meeting Excellence: 33 Tools to Lead Meetings That Get Results, by Glenn M. Parker, Robert Hoffman, ISBN-13: 978-0787982812
- Death by Meeting: A Leadership Fable...About Solving the Most Painful Problem in Business, by Patrick M. Lencioni, ISBN-13: 978-0787968052
- The Secrets of Facilitation: The S.M.A.R.T. Guide to Getting Results With Groups, by Michael Wilkinson, ISBN-13: 978-0787975784

Words and Stories – How to use words and stories to get your point across

- All Marketers Are Liars: The Power of Telling Authentic Stories in a Low-Trust World, by Seth Godin, ISBN-13: 978-1591841005
- The Story Factor (2nd Revised Edition), by Annette Simmons, Doug Lipman, ISBN-13: 978-0465078073

- The Leader's Guide to Storytelling: Mastering the Art and Discipline of Business Narrative, by Stephen Denning, ISBN-13: 978-0787976750

The Written Word – How to utilize the most overlooked written communication

- How to Say It: Choice Words, Phrases, Sentences, and Paragraphs for Every Situation, Revised Edition, by Rosalie Maggio, ISBN-13: 978-0735202344

Memos and Reports – How to develop powerful reports and memos

- The Elements of Business Writing: A Guide to Writing Clear, Concise Letters, Memos, Reports, Proposals, and Other Business Documents, by Gary Blake, Robert W. Bly, ISBN-13: 978-0020080954
- Business Grammar, Style & Usage: The Most Used Desk Reference for Articulate and Polished Business Writing and Speaking by Executives Worldwide, by Alicia Abell, ISBN-13: 978-1587620263
- Effective Business Writing :(A Guide For Those who Write On the Job) 2nd Edition Revised And Updated, by Maryann V. Piotrowski, ISBN-13: 978-0062733818

Gatekeeper Barriers – How to get client gatekeepers to help you win

- Barry Farber's Guide To Handling Sales Objections, by Barry J. Farber, ISBN-13: 978-1564147738
- Little Red Book of Selling: 12.5 Principles of Sales Greatness, by Jeffrey Gitomer, ISBN-13: 978-1885167606
- Never Eat Alone: And Other Secrets to Success, One Relationship at a Time, by Keith Ferrazzi, Tahl Raz, ISBN-13: 978-0385512053

Self Promotion – How to promote yourself to the top of your profession
- Value Forward Marketing: How to Use Thought Leadership and Return-on-Investment Calculations to Cost Effectively Turn Prospects Into Buyers by Paul R. Dimodica, ISBN-13: 978-1933598352
- 49 Marketing Secrets (That Work) to Grow Sales by Ronald Finklestein, Dennis Sommer (Contributor) ISBN-13: 978-1600372483
- The New Rules of Marketing and PR: How to Use News Releases, Blogs, Podcasting, Viral Marketing and Online Media to Reach Buyers Directly by David Meerman Scott, ISBN-13: 978-0470113455
- Guerrilla Marketing, 4th edition: Easy and Inexpensive Strategies for Making Big Profits from Your Small Business by Jay Conrad Levinson, ISBN-13: 978-0618785919

Household Name – How you can become a household name in your industry
- Sales Management Power Strategies: Building a replicable and scalable sales process by Paul R. Dimodica, ISBN-13: 978-1933598284
- Value Forward Selling: How to sell to management by Paul R. Dimodica, ISBN-13: 978-1933598314
- Good to Great: Why Some Companies Make the Leap... and Others Don't by Jim Collins ISBN-13: 978-0066620992

About The Author

Dennis Sommer is the founder and CEO of **Executive Business Advisers**, a management consulting firm specializing in sales and profit improvement.

Dennis helps companies take their business performance to the next level by showing them how to maximize sales and profit growth.

As a sales and profit improvement specialist, he understands how to make your strategy, financial management, marketing and sales work together to dramatically improve your business performance.

CEO's call Dennis to help them:
- increase sales revenue and profitability;
- improve marketing return on investment;
- reduce sales and marketing costs;
- improve financial management and business valuation;
- develop growth focused business, marketing and sales strategies.

Dennis is a successful entrepreneur, management consultant and business leader. Since 1985 he has started 2 successful growth focused companies. First, a high-tech product company. Second, a technology consulting firm. He has also held executive positions in sales, business development, operations and information technology.

Dennis is a highly sought after keynote and seminar speaker on sales, leadership and business best practices. He also provides full day customized workshops for corporate clients.

Dennis is an international author, publishing over 70 articles on sales, leadership, project management and IT management topics. He is the publisher of The Executive Adviser (www.theexecutiveadviser. com). Dennis is also a staff writer for the world's largest sales and marketing strategy newsletter called BDM News (www.bdmnews.

com) read by over 177,000 weekly subscribers in over 110 countries. He is also a staff writer for CEO Management (www. ceomanagement.com), a specialty newsletter published for senior executives.

Dennis is a contributing author for the book, *49 Marketing Secrets (that work) To Grow Sales.* His third book, *Adviser Secrets: Business Start-Up and Growth Essentials*, is also scheduled to be released soon.

How To Contact the Author

Large and small businesses have one challenge in common, limited resources to take them to the next level. Are you looking to grow your business, increase sales, or improve profitability?

Having a **trusted CEO adviser may be just what you need.**

Dennis Sommer is available for:
- CEO and Executive Team Adviser
- Business Strategy and Management Consulting
- Sales Strategy, Management and Training
- Marketing Strategy and Planning
- Professional Development Workshops
- Keynote Speaker
- Seminar Workshops
- Media Interviews

Executive Business Advisers
Sales and Profit Improvement Specialist

Toll-Free: 800-627-6512
Local: 330-676-1876
Website: www.executivebusinessadvisers.com
Speaker: www.dennissommer.com
Newsletter: www.theexecutiveadviser.com

Added Strength
Executive Business Advisers is a partner of the Value Forward Network, one of the world's largest sales and management consulting groups focused on helping companies increase corporate revenue generation.

Download Your Client Communication Toolkit

A client communication toolkit for those who are ready to implement the tactics and strategies laid out in this book. The toolkit includes communication templates, forms and assessments. All the forms and scripts described in this book are included. You will also receive a self assessment questionnaire for each chapter.

If you would like more information, please contact us toll-free 1-800-627-6512. Or, go to www.executivebusinessadvisers.com and select the "Products" tab to see a complete list of the products available.

Other Services by Dennis Sommer

Inspire and Motivate Your Audience
Beyond Their Expectations

Have Dennis speak at you next event!

If you're planning a conference, seminar, meeting, retreat, or training class this year, exceed your audience expectations by providing a speaker and topic that is educational, stimulating and motivational. The hands-on seminars provided by Dennis Sommer focus on current hot topics most important to your audience. Each seminar is unique and customized for your event based on the audience profile and their most critical concerns. Dennis will inspire and motivate the audience while delivering sound actionable information that will improve their performance.

If you would like more information, please contact Dennis toll-free 1-800-627-6512. Or, go to www.executivebusinessadvisers.com and www.dennissommer.com .

Sign-up for a FREE - CEO Newsletter

The Executive Adviser

Each month, we bring you proven tactical and strategic sales, marketing and operations techniques to help you maximize your sales and profit growth. Currently read by C-Level executives, presidents, business owners, vice presidents, and sales executives worldwide.

To sign-up, go to www.theexecutiveadviser.com.